FINDING THE FORK IN THE ROAD

FINDING THE FORK IN THE ROAD

The Art of Maximizing
the Potential of
Business Partnerships

LINDA FINKLE

Published by Advantage, Charleston, South Carolina.
Member of Advantage Media Group.

ADVANTAGE is a registered trademark and the Advantage colophon is a trademark of Advantage Media Group, Inc.

Printed in the United States of America.

ISBN: 978-1-59932-217-9
LCCN: 2010908978

This publication is designed to provide accurate and authoritative information in regard to the subject matter covered. It is sold with the understanding that the publisher is not engaged in rendering legal, accounting, or other professional services. If legal advice or other expert assistance is required, the services of a competent professional person should be sought.

Most Advantage Media Group titles are available at special quantity discounts for bulk purchases for sales promotions, premiums, fundraising, and educational use. Special versions or book excerpts can also be created to fit specific needs.

For more information, please write: Special Markets, Advantage Media Group, P.O. Box 272, Charleston, SC 29402 or call 1.866.775.1696.

Visit us online at **advantagefamily**.com

Table of Contents

Partnerships are a powerful way to do business, but they aren't meant to be until-death-do-us-part entities. This book will tell you how your partnership can reach the fork in the road, the place where you attain maximum profitability and satisfaction, where you can end the partnership properly. The end might mean retirement of a partner, sale of the business to other partners, or a merger or acquisition. Look for tips on how to read this book and use the tools and assessments.

First, let's define a partnership, and then look at the benefits of having a partner or partners to share, for example, expenses, workload, expertise, setbacks and successes. Partnerships come in all sizes, from 2 to 22 to 222, and all have challenges. Learn the top seven partnership success factors and use the checklist to determine your reasons for partnering.

A partnership is like other relationships: You need to get to know each other before proceeding. Find out where everyone stands on work, operational and communication styles; goals; values; expenditures; ownership and roles. Use the checklist of 7 keys to determine fit, but never force a fit. Learn the qualities of good partners and some scenarios for dealing with differences.

Take a preventive approach to problems – and know that you will have problems. Pointers are provided on the issues and potential difficulties to take into account and discuss, as are the top 10 reasons why partnerships don't realize the fork in the road.

Compensation leads the list of partnership challenges, but it's more than salary. Other considerations include benefits, expenses, bonuses, retirement packages, and annuities for sweat equity. Questions are provided to determine what's fair and equitable.

Family businesses are a different type of partnership. They have both the emotional attachments of personal relationships and the business component. By the numbers: 6 things that make family businesses unique; 11 challenges that family partnerships face; and 7 keys to a successful family partnership. If you are aware of what to expect, you can adopt both preventive and prescriptive approaches to managing the challenges.

Here are 10 situations that you might have to handle, among them: Everyone wants to be equal; a partner isn't satisfied with a role, but no others are available; being on-call at a medical practice; a partner reaches the Peter Principle; or the founder is unable to give up control.

Be aware of 9 common warning signs of problems, and a preventative approach you can take. The checklist can indicate how troubled your partnership relationship might be. Beyond that, 8 distress signals of worsening conditions.

Sometimes, differences are simply too vast and the partnership needs to dissolve. It's not failure; the path you have each chosen has diverged and it's time to go your separate ways. It's important to get past the hurt and anger, and think about what you have learned. What's in store for the partner who stays and the impact on the business.

Congratulations! Your vision for your partnership has been realized. You have reached the point of maximum profitability and satisfaction for the partners, and now you will be able to end it properly. Some scenarios for finding the fork: retirement, buyout, sale or merger of business.

Introduction

Millions of smart and talented business people co-own private companies, family businesses and business partnerships. Launching them is relatively easy; keeping them together is never easy. Business partnerships have a sky-high failure rate; more than 50% of them fail. That's a staggering statistic, and doesn't account for the partnerships that may be financially successful even though the partners don't get along. They believe they have no option but to "grin and bear it." This approach means partners can suffer costly emotional and economic disputes, leading to losses that can never be recouped. And those losses go beyond the bottom line. The toll that contentious partnerships can take on the individuals, their families, the employees, and even customers is enormous. While they may not be quantifiable, these costs are as catastrophic as financial costs.

In order for partnerships to flourish beyond being profitable, partners must explore how to create a shared vision, establish compatibility, apply ground rules, build durable relationships, foster trust and measure progress, as well as learn how to handle change together as a unit. Next to marriage, a business partnership is the most intense and collaborative-dependent and interdependent relationship you can have. And just like marriage, establishing the partnership is just the first step. Building a sustainable, thriving business relationship takes work, patience and commitment.

Unlike marriages, however, partnerships are not meant to be till-death-do-you-part. That's not always so bad. After all, partnerships, like most things that come together, must eventually come apart. Take a look around. Buildings, civilizations, machines, even things in our natural surroundings came together by man or physics, but they all change and will ultimately give way to something else.

But don't think of this as a negative dynamic. Without it, progress would be impossible. Once you understand and accept this as a law of nature you will be able to shift your focus from building a partnership that stands the test of time to building a partnership so that it will end properly. You want to focus on building your partnership to the point of *maximum profitability* and *satisfaction for the partners*, and then end it, understanding that it has achieved its purpose and goal and that to continue it would be to diminish its value.

Think about this for a second. If you come together as partners with the expectation and knowledge that you are building something to reach the tipping point, that place where profits have been maximized and individual satisfaction of the partners is at its highest point, then your collective focus is on this goal. It provides the anchor, the place to come back to when things go off course or when divergent paths are options. Your goal then is to find the fork in the road, the point in time when you will separate as partners. The separation might be a buyout, a merger or even the sale of the business; the cause of the separation is not the point. The point is to build the business with *the goal of finding the fork in the road* – and when that happens, you'll know it's time to end the partnership, and will do it properly.

A couple of notes to the reader: This book is not about how to form a legal partnership. Please see an attorney for advice on legal structure, shareholders' agreements or any other legal needs. Laws vary according to location. This book is about the *people side of partnerships* … what works, what doesn't and what to do about it. While members of any partnership can benefit from reading this book, my focus is on partnerships of 25 or fewer. Larger partnerships, strategic alliances, joint ventures, medical practices and the like have many of the same challenges outlined in the book; however, they have many others that I don't cover. While I offer one chapter on family businesses, please be aware that family businesses have their own dynamics that could fill an entire book. The focus of the family business chapter is simply to provide a high-level view of family businesses and their unique demands.

How to read this book: Read it front to back, back to front, or pick out the chapters that apply to you. While the chapters connect to one another and follow a format, there is nothing wrong with reading the chapters that have the most application to you. If you are thinking about a partnership but aren't yet in one, I suggest you start at the beginning and go chapter by chapter.

Finally, throughout the book you will find assessments and other tools to help you better understand your partner or partners, the relationship and/or what's getting in the way of achieving your goals. You and your partner(s) should take them and compare notes. I'll bet you'll find the results enlightening. Many of the charts, checklists and other forms found throughout the book are on our website, www.findingtheforkintheroad.com/download (The password is FORK) and are available for download. There are also other resources on our website that are not listed in the book. Another tool you may find useful is the ProScan® assessment. The ProScan® by Professional DynaMetric Programs is a development tool unlike any you may be familiar with. Not only does it accurately assess your individual, preferred work style, it examines the unique combination of traits and factors that affect how you work most effectively. When I work with partnerships or teams, I have everyone involved take this assessment. It's an amazing tool that helps you identify differences in work style, logic style (how you approach challenges or situations) and even your leadership and communication styles. And it offers so much more than that.

Since 2000 I have worked with numerous business partnerships. I have helped them navigate through the challenges and find solutions to their most difficult problems. At times I have worked with individuals to determine whether they should join forces and become partners. With other partnerships, I have worked closely with them to dissolve the partnership and/or end the relationship to find their fork in the road. Several of the partnerships were family business, and working with them offered me insights into the unique situations they face. I've run businesses for more than 30 years and have had a partner myself. My expertise in the area of communication, knowledge of businesses and understanding of relationships provides not just the theoretical understanding of the issues, but one-on-one experience working with partnerships.

I hope you find this book useful. If you have a question not answered by the book feel free to write, call or e-mail me:

Linda Finkle
1752 Glastonberry Road
Potomac, MD 20854
301-315-2420
Linda@FindingtheForkIntheRoad.com

CHECKLIST 1

Are you partnering because …

1. You need to share the workload?

2. You want to increase your capacity and revenues?

3. You want to have someone to talk to?

4. You want to reduce personal financial risk?

5. You hate going it alone?

6. There are skills you need that you don't have?

7. Two heads are better than one?

8. Everyone's doing it?

9. Your attorney or accountant suggested it was a good idea?

10. You and a friend (or family member) have a great idea?

11. You have no clue, but why not?

Know why you are partnering before saying yes. There are lots of appealing aspects to partnerships; know why you are saying yes.

Does Size Matter?

Does the size of the partnership have a positive impact on its success or, conversely, on the chances of its survival? Answering this question is like predicting whether a marriage will survive for 30 years or end in divorce a few years after the honeymoon. Partnerships, like marriages, have an intimacy that can strengthen the union or destroy it. Remember, however, you are not building a partnership to last forever. You are building the partnership to reach the maximum point of success and then end it appropriately. Survival of the partnership needs to be viewed through this lens.

There is no greater survival rate for companies that have dozens or even hundreds of partners than for those that have only two. Law firms are a good example. Many of the largest exist because they merged with another firm, and that new firm merged with yet another firm. Along the way, many of the partners from the initial firm left to form their own firms or join another. Yes, the firm still exists, but not the original partnership. Same with sports teams – the teams still exist, but the players change. As the ancient Greek philosopher Heraclitus declared more than 2,500 years ago, "Things change." Such is true with partnerships.

Any size partnership will have challenges. Two is a difficult number, regardless of the split of ownership. Three offers the opportunity for two ganging up on one. Twenty means the potential for 20 different opinions, ideas and personal interests entering into discussions. One hundred means less liability for each partner, but also less input into decision-making.

Whether your partnership is two, 20, 200 or 2,000, it can be terrific *yet* have pitfalls. When you add elements or change the quantity of the ingredients in chemistry, something different is created. Such is true with partnerships. Changing the number of partners or the people who are partners changes the dynamics, and though the new partnership may resemble the original one, it will be different. This is simply part of the laws of nature.

Partnerships stay together for any number of reasons, but how many are fulfilling, happy and productive? Statistics say not too many. I don't mean the normal ups and downs of all relationships; I'm referring to the partners who would break up if they had a choice, or thought they did.

Can you build a partnership that works financially and is emotionally fulfilling so that you reach the fork in the road? If you are in a partnership already, are you destined to remain in challenging, difficult and often unpleasant relationships, or can this partnership be saved?

The answer is a resounding yes! Yes, you can build a partnership that works. Yes, your partnership can be saved! Yes, you can move your current problematic partnership to a positive relationship. Your partnership does not have to end prematurely with angst and emotional and financial upheaval for everyone. And no, you don't need to suffer in silence, grin and bear it or remain in a relationship fraught with disagreements, discord or frustration. Through the rest of this book, I'm going to show you how to build your partnership to reach the goal of getting to the fork in the road.

Top Seven Partnership Success Factors

1. Shared values, vision and goals, and a process to get there

2. Measuring progress and handling change as a unit

3. Each partners' needs and expectations are addressed

4. Effective communication strategies in place

5. Readiness of each partner

6. Success of the business is more important than any individual needs

7. Unrelenting focus on building the partnership so it can end properly

Chapter 2
The Importance of Fit in the Business Partnership

"It's rare to find a business partner who is selfless. If you are lucky, it happens once in a lifetime." – *Michael Eisner*

How to Determine Good Fit

Creating and maintaining a successful partnership takes a lot of work. Partnerships become dysfunctional for any number of reasons, and we will address many of those in future chapters. However, poor fit ranks at the top of the list, because it can ruin a partnership before it gets off the ground. Fit isn't as much about shared financial goals as it is about meshing personal and professional goals.

Think of this in terms of any other relationship. What if you married someone who wanted four children, a house in the city and a lifestyle of travel, possessions and showy capitalism, yet you wanted one or maybe two children, a house in the suburbs and a simple life? The mix of these two sets of goals would cause tremendous challenges in the relationship. A business relationship without shared vision and shared goals is no different.

In personal relationships, love does not conquer all if your vision and goals are vastly different. In business, financial success does not conquer all if you don't have shared vision and goals. In personal relationships, being in love makes the differences more palatable. In business relationships, financial success may make the differences tolerable, but why would you want to settle for tolerable? Those differences will eventually ruin the partnership and cause it to end prematurely. Imagine what your life could be like and what your business could achieve if your vision, values and goals were in line with your partner's.

It's so easy to overlook the importance of taking the time to really get to know each other and make sure that your personal and professional goals mesh. Two or more people want to get together to build something. They have a shared vision for the product, service and financial goals of the company. What else matters? Actually, a lot matters. Let's take a look at some of the personal and professional goals that need to be discussed before partners join forces. Some may seem like little things to you, but it's often the little things that eat away at relationships.

CHECKLIST 2

Seven keys to determine fit.

1. **Compatible work ethic:** Determine whether you both envision working long, hard hours to accomplish the goals. Are you both willing to do whatever it takes to get the job done?

2. **Shared vision:** Do you both see a similar outcome? If everything were working perfectly, what would that look like?

3. **Alignment of values**: Do you share consistent and similar values? Each of you list your top five and compare.

4. **Integrity:** Do you both have the same views and principles?

5. **Dealing with conflict:** How do you each deal with conflict? Are your styles compatible?

6. **Trust:** Do you trust each other based on a gut emotional reaction or a past relationship?

7. **Sense of humor:** Can you both laugh, be lighthearted and have fun?

Where Do You Stand?

Before you decide to partner with someone, it's critical to determine where you and your partner agree on issues and where you disagree. Being in agreement on everything is not essential. Knowing where you aren't is essential, however, as it provides the platform for discussion. The differences aren't and will not be the problem. The problem is not realizing there are differences, ignoring them or taking the time to determine how you will manage through them. We've provided you examples of situations that we have found to be "the big ones," the ones that most often cause conflict.

Work styles: Discuss work hours, whether work can bleed into personal time, how does family mesh with work, vacation time, travel, handling personal issues during company time, do you want to spend time together outside the office, amount of work time versus play time each wants, work load and other work-style considerations.

Individual professional goals: What do you each want for yourself from this business? Can you both achieve your goals, or will one achieve at the expense of the other?

Values: Family, money, status, opportunity, structure, harmony, leadership and a whole host of other issues. A discussion of values will reveal potential challenges or hurdles you will face in the relationship.

Family members: Do you agree on hiring family members?

Communication styles: Is one of you conflict-averse and the other a talker? Do you agree on how much you will share with employees? What are you willing to share with each other? What are you not willing to share?

Financial expenditures: Do you agree on how lavish the office space will be, what technology is needed, where you spend money and don't? What about income? Will you set aside all or part of your salary and reinvest it in the business?

Ownership: Do you need to be equals? How do you make this decision? What if one person puts in financial equity and the other sweat equity?

Long-term business goals: Is this a lifestyle business (operated more for your enjoyment or satisfaction) or one that will build substantive value enabling you to eventually sell? Either goal can get you to the fork in the road but how you get there may be different.

Operational styles: Structure, process, procedures, metrics, accountability and more. Do you agree on these matters or are you polar opposites?

Roles and responsibilities: Will you both do everything or have defined roles? Will you honor your roles' boundaries? Will one of you be the face of the company while the other runs the back office? Do you agree on the roles each will have?

All of these topics and more need to be discussed long before you agree to join forces and build a business together. While it's critical to be in agreement on some, (e.g., long-term business goals) others may not be as critical. However, it is essential to understand each other's expectations to ward off many problems later on.

Our website has a Values exercise you can download. You and a potential partner should independently take the assessment and compare results. Areas that show where you aren't in alignment need to be discussed, even small things. Don't assume "things will work themselves out once we start making money." They won't. When we are excited about the possibilities, we believe anything and everything can be overcome. Now is the time to talk through the differences, find points of compromise and determine how you will handle the differences. Otherwise, over time they will eat away at the relationship and the business. The deterioration of the relationship will interfere with your reaching the primary goal of arriving at that fork in the road, that place of maximum profits, potential and satisfaction. Know what has the potential to be explosive and is critical before mentally or legally signing on the dotted line together.

What's Likely to Happen When...

- **Values are significantly different:** Some differences are inevitable. You may place emphasis on status and recognition or operational considerations, while your partner doesn't care. Depending on the roles you each hold in the company, this may actually be a plus. But other values differences are not so easily dismissed. A mismatch in financial needs or beliefs around money, work/life balance and leadership styles can cause havoc. When you discuss values and realize you are incongruent, take the time to determine how you will manage through these differences.

- **Long-term business goals are dissimilar:** This may or may not relate to values. Realize that if you want a lifestyle business and your partner wants to build a business to sell, then your relationship is doomed from the start. This will cause considerable challenges and problems and will not likely be resolvable.

- **Communication styles are worlds apart or too similar:** Communication will be the key to everything that works and everything that doesn't work in your relationship and in your company. If one or both of you avoids discussions where you likely won't agree, is conflict-averse or has a "say nothing till things are out of control" style, then solving problems, having difficult discussions and coming to agreement will be painful at best.

- **The difficulties and risks in partnering are ignored:** Any new relationship comes with difficulties and risks. Assuming that they just don't matter or they'll go away once you make tons of money, or ignoring them altogether may feel right at the moment, but long-term they will bubble up and cause trouble. Make sure you agree as to the difficulties and risks associated with this new relationship and how you will handle them when they inevitably occur.

These clearly are not the only considerations. However, if you can't come to agreement on these, the relationship is doomed to fail. That doesn't mean the business will fail; it just means that the relationship will consistently and continually be fraught with problems, angst and frustration. And who wants to go to work every day having to deal with relationship problems with your partner? Talk through these issues and determine whether you are in alignment. And if you are not, determine how you will handle the disparity in how you think.

A Case Study: Two Brothers

For several years I worked with two brothers who were partners. They hired me to help them stabilize their revenues, hire more effectively and work through the challenges that existed between them. It quickly became apparent that the business challenges were due to misaligned values and work ethics of the brothers. Both wanted the benefits of financial success, yet were not willing to put in the long hours and make the necessary adjustments to their personal lives to ensure the financial outcome. The results were constant disagreements, lots of finger-pointing, blame, accusations, hurt feelings, high emotions and enormous stress for the individual brothers, their families and the company's employees. Ultimately, the partnership dissolved and one brother bought out the other. However, months of resentment, emotional upheaval and threats of litigation followed until it was all resolved. This showcases the importance of the having similar values, goals and visions or discussing how you will manage through what is different.

The Unavoidable Partnership

What do you do if you have no choice of a partner? Maybe it's a family business. Maybe you are in an established partnership and the other partners vote in a partner you wouldn't. There is no easy resolution to this situation.

If you are in an established partnership, then it's likely you have already accepted the fact that you may be out-voted at times. The big question to answer is: How often is it OK for you to be out-voted? Should you find yourself consistently disagreeing with your partners on individuals who are approved as partners, then it's time to ask yourself the bigger question: Is this indicative of other differences in how you and your partners see things? Maybe it's significant and maybe not.

What if you are joining a family business? Just remember you don't have to join a family business; the choice is yours. However, if you do so, go in with your eyes wide open. Adding family dynamics to a business relationship creates its own set of challenges. That doesn't mean it can't or won't work. It just means that you have to be aware of how the "family stuff" will affect the relationship. For more on family businesses, see Chapter 11. If you are ready to join a family business or are considering partnering with a family member, read that chapter before making a decision.

If the Shoe Doesn't Fit, Don't Buy It

Have you ever bought a pair of shoes that aren't really comfortable or don't fit exactly right, but you liked the style or needed the color or the price was right? You convinced yourself that they would get comfortable over time or that you didn't have another option. Yet they never got more comfortable and you quit wearing them. Sooner or later you gave them away or threw them out.

The same is true with partnerships. The uncomfortable ones do not get more comfortable over time or fit better. You may want it to work, even knowing there are significant differences and challenges, and that's admirable. You may try to convince yourself that the fit will improve over time, that financial success will mask the differences or that you can suck it up. And maybe you can. But recognize that the probability is you will be sucking it up for the rest of your relationship.

On the other hand, you may decide to say no and not try to force the partnership to fit. Can you maintain a relationship with this person if you say no to the partnership? What if you are family, close friends, business colleagues or have a long-time relationship? Will saying no destroy the existing relationship? It may, and accepting this as a possibility is something to consider when making your go/no-go decision. To quote John D. Rockefeller, "A friendship founded on business is a good deal better than a business founded on friendship."

Qualities of individuals who make good partners

1. They foster trust and are fiercely loyal to others.

2. They look for the lessons in every situation, whether it works or doesn't, and see how to apply them.

3. Blame isn't a word in their vocabulary. They are hard wired to accept responsibility for themselves.

4. They are able to laugh at themselves and challenging situations.

5. They are able to keep their wits about them when everything around them seems to be falling apart.

6. They apply ground rules equally and consistently.

Chapter 3
The Nature of Partnerships

As mentioned in Chapter 2, partnerships not only take a lot of work to be successful, they can become dysfunctional for any number of reasons. The first step is, of course the fit. Once you determine that the fit exists, the next step is to consider the factors that may cause friction or discord and discuss in advance how you will handle them. I call this the "preventive approach."

The problems are not the problem. Assuming there will be no problems is not only foolish, but is in itself a problem. How we handle problems when they arise makes the difference between a successful partnership and one destined for frustration, disappointment and strife. Talking about how you will handle these situations when they arise won't eliminate the problems, but it will provide you the platform to handle them so emotions don't rule the conversations. At least as important is that advance discussions will align your expectations with reality. Often a situation goes from a simple problem to World War III because of the surprise factor. We are surprised that the situation occurred at all, and that interferes with our thinking and ability to work through the problem. Don't wait till these issues occur before determining how to handle them. Have this discussion either before you commit to one another or at least early on in the relationship.

What Kinds of Issues/Potential Problems Should You Take into Account and Discuss?

- **Your excitement and passion will wane.** What happens when one or both of you lose your excitement for the business or even the partnership? It's going to happen, but it doesn't mean disaster. Have you ever taken on a big project, perhaps redoing your garden. You plan, buy the plants, dig the holes, plant the trees/shrubs and flowers, fertilize, mulch and wait for the garden to bloom. And while you are waiting weeds grow and a couple of shrubs die. Do you lose your excitement for the garden and wonder whether you made a mistake? No, you realize this is just part of the process you need to go through to enjoy the beauty of your garden. Remember the primary goal of your partnership is building it so it ends well. Along the way you'll have the weeds and thorny parts, all necessary to enjoy the end result.

- **You are friends or family and assume that when personal situations occur the other party will understand and accept whatever happens.** That could be anything such as childcare challenges, divorce, death, illness, financial problems, etc. Because of the closeness of your relationship there is an unstated expectation that the other person will understand and tolerate whatever actions you take, even if it affects the business. Isaac Newton stated that for every action there is an equal and opposite reaction. Every action you take and decision you make as an individual affects how successfully and quickly the partnership gets to the fork in the road.

- **Not having clearly defined roles and responsibilities.** Often partnerships begin with all parties doing everything. You are, after all a team, and team members chip in to help one another. Yet at some point the business will grow, making a separation of roles and responsibilities necessary. Define now what role each will take, why it makes sense and come to agreement.

- **How decisions get made.** If ownership is equal, who makes the final decision if there is a disagreement? If the ownership is not equal, does the partner with the most equity decide? If you have no other discussion, have the one on how decisions get made. Down the road, it will save lots of frustration, hurt feelings, negative energy and time.

- **Plans for communication.** Communication is critical for success in any relationship. I firmly believe that everything that works and everything that doesn't work in our lives, both personally and professionally, is about communication. Plan for how you are going to communicate, the frequency, on what subjects you will communicate, what you expect of each other and how to get the communication back on track when it goes awry. As George Bernard Shaw said, "The single biggest problem in communication is the illusion that it has taken place."

- **The focus is on building the business and not on other critical factors that affect the partnership.** It's so easy to focus on generating revenues, building the client base and profitability, that it's easy to forget the relationship. The relationship and the business are intertwined. Thinking today about the care and feeding of the relationship, not just the business, will keep your eye on how interconnected the two are.

- **No real business plan from inception.** You don't have to create a full-fledged plan that you would present to the bank or an investor to secure funding. But you do need to discuss and create together a general outline and plan for the direction of the business. What are the short- and long-term goals, how will you get there, what resources do you need … all the broad brushstrokes of a business plan. Without this discussion you may find yourself going in many different directions that may or may not lead one or more partners where they expected to go.

In upcoming chapters we will discuss many of these topics in detail, both the preventive approach mentioned here, and the prescriptive approach we will outline. Communication will be the theme throughout the rest of this book. I'll show you how communication can be a barrier to success or a tool to build your company or revolutionize the one you have already. You'll learn how poor communication, miscommunication or no communication can be the root of every problem. You might not even realize that the problems, issues and challenges that occur in your company are really due to communication. They are often attributed to something else – bad attitude, unrealistic deadlines, inadequate hiring, and too many things going on at the same time … the list goes on. Relationships are no different. You may attribute the problems with your partner to his or her personal life, lack of skills, attitudes … this list goes on. Yet in most, if not all, situations the issue is really communication. You just don't realize it.

Individuals need to focus on how to build a partnership so that it will end properly, when it has reached its greatest point of profitability, potential and satisfaction for the partners. The single biggest factor that will prevent this from occurring is poor or ineffective communication.

Do you know the top 10 reasons why partnerships don't realize the fork in the road?

1. Unrealistic or unclear expectations

2. Power clashes

3. No solid business plan to build the business and/or no processes created to get there

4. Forgotten agreements

5. Absence of metrics and accountability

6. Poorly or ill-defined roles and responsibilities

7. Underestimating the difficulties, risks and challenges in partnering

8. Lack of trust

9. Incompatible work ethics/styles or values

10. Mismatch of communication styles so great it prevents partners from working through problems

Chapter 4
Stages of Partnership Development

What to Expect

Companies go through developmental stages, teams go through developmental stages and partnerships go through developmental stages. Any time we bring two or more people together, the relationship will go through changes over time. This can be disconcerting. Like marriages, when the relationship becomes stormy, people begin to question it. What does this mean? Should we throw in the towel and end our partnership? Can we get through this? It must be them, if only they could change. And so on.

Search the Internet and you'll find that businesses go through a variety of stages. The authors label them differently, suggest there are anywhere from four to seven stages, and describe the length of each stage and what happens at each slightly differently. What is consistent, however, is the fact that businesses have a developmental life cycle that is not too different from the developmental stages of people. Often the developmental stages of people are defined as infancy, childhood, adolescence, young adulthood, adulthood and, inevitably, death. Business developmental stages are often defined in similar terms. For the purpose of this book we will define these stages as: start-up, growth, maturity, decline and revival.

Your partnership relationship, just like your business, will go through developmental stages. Some may be exciting and exhilarating, and others will feel like just darn hard work. You'll ask yourself a hundred times over, "Why am I doing this?" At times you'll even forget what you liked about your partners and why you wanted to join forces with them. All of this is typical, normal and expected. I'm not suggesting that there may not come a time when the partnerships dissolves, but we are way far from that point. What I am saying is that just because the partnership is rocky, the bloom has fallen off the rose and the relationship has changed does not mean the partnership (or the business) is doomed for failure.

This is the perfect time to refocus on the primary goal of the partnership. Remember I mentioned that throughout the partnership you will face times when you are in the woods and don't know which path to take. Or you may find that you and your partner are on different paths. You can be drawn back together by resuming the conversation on the goal of the partnership. Coming back to this place, this goal will ground you and help you when you get lost or uncertain.

Sit back and relax a bit. Read about the stages of partnership development. Assess where your partnership is and realize that this relationship, like all other relationships, will change, develop and, you hope, grow over time.

Defining the Stages

Consider where your partnership is in relation to the stage of your business. While there is no direct correlation between your relationship and the stage of the business, you will find some parallels. The hard truth is, when a business is struggling financially it will affect the thoughts, feelings and emotions of the people involved in the business. It's easy to blame your partners for what's not working, and your interaction with them will change as a result. When the business is thriving, we are typically more tolerant of our partners and their foibles. What's curious, however, is that a thriving business does not necessarily guarantee a positive relationship between the partners. Nor do we typically find partners patting one another on the back and giving credit to the others for the success. This is more about human nature than the stage of the partnership. It is worth noting, however, that some typical reactions, feelings and emotions bubble up at specific stages. Recognizing and understanding them helps you manage them more easily.

CHECKLIST 3

At which stage is your partnership?

Check which stage you think you are in before reading the descriptions.

Stage 1: Inception, start-up and launch

Stage 2: Go-go-go, growth, eruption

Stage 3: Maturity, institutionalization, established

Stage 4: Decline, deterioration, downhill slide

Stage 5: Revival, action, regeneration

Stage 1: Inception, Start-up and Launch

Characteristics:

- Excitement, enthusiasm and anticipation rule the day

- Hard work and intense activity

- Focus is on making the business successful

At the inception stage you actually will find a direct correlation between the relationship and the stage of the business. Everyone is excited, passionate and full of hope. There is so much to do to launch the business and take it to the next stage. Each partner is working hard, activity is intense, excitement is high, laughter is frequent and partners work to understand each other and work as a unit. Egos take a back seat to building a successful business. While the hours may be long and the list of to-dos never seems to end, the anticipation of the future and your individual enthusiasm for what you are creating together overshadows everything else. Each partner has idiosyncrasies, quirks and shortcomings. But at this stage you are indifferent to them, ignore them altogether or maybe just don't see them. Enthusiasm is boundless, fear does not hamper progress, confidence is the operative word and partners are obsessive, almost zealot-like in their pursuit of success.

Everything seems to work and anything that doesn't is not attributed to the individual but to something else – incorrect thinking, poor planning, flawed marketing plan, any number of factors. No one lays blame, no one takes exception to what the other is doing or not doing. The focus is purely on moving the business forward and what must be done together to make this happen.

Stage 2: Go-Go-Go, Growth, Eruption

Characteristics:

- Recognition that it's hard work and will continue to be

- Individual personalities become the focal point

- Disenchantment, restlessness and frustration prevail

Your partnership (and business) has made it through the inception, start-up and launch stage. Revenues and customers are increasing, opportunities appear endless. This success brings with it new issues and challenges, and the initial excitement and fervor begin to wane as you recognize this is lots of hard work and the end is not in sight. Politeness begins to wear off, your partner's shortcomings and inadequacies are front and center, and disagreement becomes the norm.

During this stage, the who, what and how become the focal point. Who is going to do what, what decisions get made, who decides what and how things get done. Control often becomes a primary issue between partners as you struggle through all the decisions and details, and come to recognize that while success is still within your vision, the path to get there looks longer and longer. This stage is often the most difficult for both the business and the partners to weather, but is necessary for healthy relationships. Don't ignore this stage or assume anything negative; it's just a stage of development the partnership needs to go through. Remember the garden analogy I used earlier? It's fitting for this stage. Acknowledge this as a natural development. This is a good time to revisit why you started this business, the goals and aspirations you each had, and why you joined forces in the first place.

Stage 3: Maturity, Institutionalization, Established

Characteristics:

- Recognition of the importance of structure, processes and procedures

- Focus is on problem-solving and solidifying the business

- Decisions made based on facts and information

- Partners work together as a unit

At this stage your business and your partnership have matured and leveled. You have recognized your differences and have dealt with them and have established the need for institutionalizing all internal structures, processes and procedures. Ground rules and formal procedures that were overlooked in the beginning are now taken more seriously and implemented. Problem-solving is the focus, and partners examine what is working, what is not and where intervention is needed. Whether it is a new process, procedure, additional staff and/or leadership or a change in the organizational structure, etc., attention is placed on solidifying the business.

Partners begin to ask themselves and one another different types of questions. While control is still a consideration, it is not control for control's sake any longer, or a result of blame. In this stage, control is about what the business needs to make it run like a well-oiled machine. Fundamental to making decisions is information, and partners come to realize they either don't have enough or the right information to make key decisions. More time is now spent on specific topics than on generating ideas and big-picture thinking.

Partners hunker down to make things happen and spend more time on decision-making.

Partners have come through the Go-Go-Go stage and have learned to work through their differences. Emotional conflicts are reduced. Once again, partners come together as a unit to take the business to the next stage. A renewed excitement erupts; blame and judgment are not part of conversations. The partners focus time and energy on decisions and what needs to be accomplished.

Stage 4: Decline, Deterioration, Downhill Slide

Characteristics:
- Revenues flatten or decline

- Requires partners to work together harmoniously and as a unit

- Emotional energy needs to shift to revitalizing the business

- Important to examine lessons learned

As focus is placed in Stage 3 on institutionalizing internal structures, less focus is given to business development, watching the big picture and seeing beyond what is happening in the company at this moment. In Stage 4, customer growth is leveling off or declining; expenses are significant as staff, technology, office space, etc. are added to manage the infrastructure that was created in Stage 3; and revenue growth is not keeping pace with expenses. It's common that a key customer leaves, and partners realize this customer was a significant portion of their revenue. Now they are vulnerable. Fear, judgment, accusations and blame take hold. Partnership relationships may again become strained as the business works to ride out the storm.

All businesses go through this stage eventually. The length of this stage is determined by how well the partners handle these changes as a unit. Now is not the time to point fingers, criticize and condemn each other for what happened or what isn't working. Keep your emotions in check and shift that emotional energy toward revitalization of the business. Slow down and take the time to determine what is working brilliantly and what areas need strengthening. Examine the lessons you have learned and determine how they can be used to shape your business as you rebuild. The longer you and your partners fight, cast aspersions, criticize and focus on who is to blame, the longer it will take to come through Stage 4. Put your attention on what's next instead of who got us here.

Stage 4 can be difficult and emotionally challenging for the partners. It requires partners to work together harmoniously to revitalize the business, and each partner has to be invigorated to make this happen. It is, however, the most positive of all stages thus far. It makes the partnership relationship stronger and thus the business stronger. Partners become a unit when it comes to problem-solving, decision-making and setting direction. Lessons learned in Stage 4 will be used to head off future issues before they become problems. Attention is once again placed on the how to build the partnership so it will come to an end appropriately. All good news!

Stage 5: Revival, Action, Regeneration

Characteristics:

- Partners reengaged, optimistic and activity is high

- Idealism and naivety is nonexistent

- High level of trust and respect for each other

- At times the partnership ends

You've reached the final stage of development. In Stage 5, partners are more proactive and productive. Effectiveness and focus are the norm. Like Stage 1, excitement is again high, activity is intense and partners are working hard. Unlike Stage 1, partners are not idealistic and naïve. They accept one another, recognize their differences and have come to appreciate those differences and what the partners bring to the business and relationship. They have renewed focus, energy, trust and respect for each other. Optimism is high and partners feel and act empowered.

Sometimes, however, the emotional toll of Stage 4 results in one or more partners believing they can't work together or their differences are too overwhelming and the only solution is to end the relationship. If that happens, take steps to dissolve the partnership in a professional and businesslike manner. In Chapter 14 we address dissolving the relationship. Suffice it to say, however, it will be challenging. Bringing feelings into the discussions is costly to all parties; leave your feelings and emotions out of discussions and focus on what's best for each partner and the business.

One point to remember: A partner's leaving or the dissolution of the partnership may in fact be not only a positive, but also necessary. It opens up the possibility to new opportunities and unexpected outcomes. Keep in mind you came together to build a partnership knowing there would be an end. This is just one of the potential endings.

Dynamics Change As Partners Are Added or Leave

Partners may go through these stages many times over throughout their relationship. With the addition of new partners or as partners leave, the dynamics will change. It's like cooking: If you change one ingredient in your recipe the result will be different. Different does not connote bad, it just means different. You may be in the middle of Stage 3 when you add another partner or two, and suddenly you find yourself thrown back into Stage 2 or accelerated into Stage 4. A partner may leave unexpectedly and suddenly you shift from Stage 5 back to Stage 4. Each person you add will change the dynamics of the relationship and thus likely dramatically shift where you are in your development.

Don't let this throw you off-center. It's typical. It's natural to go to the mindset of "Oh, no, how did this happen?" or "We'll never survive!" Allow yourself to think these thoughts; just don't wallow in self-pity or let these thoughts keep you stuck. Determine where you are now and what you need to do to move forward. This is a prime opportunity to revisit goals, vision and values.

CHECKLIST 4

At which stage is your partnership?

Now that you have read the descriptions, at which stage do you see your partnership? Is it the same as what you thought before reading the descriptions?

Stage 1: Inception, start-up and launch

Stage 2: Go-go-go, growth, eruption

Stage 3: Maturity, institutionalization, established

Stage 4: Decline, deterioration, downhill slide

Stage 5: Revival, action, regeneration

Some final thoughts about stages of partnership development:

1. As new people (not just partners) join the team or leave the organization, interactions will change, as will the overall dynamics. Whether this throws you into another stage of development depends on a variety of factors, and you can't control, predict or plan for how to manage through it, except to ensure you have open communication channels in place. Accept this as the natural course of development. Power comes from learning from each success or failure.

2. The length of each stage is not predictable. You can't force a stage to happen, bypass a stage or forcefully push through a stage. Infants crawl before they stand, they stand before they walk and they walk before they run. Eventually they all crawl, stand, walk and run, but the timing is unpredictable. My older daughter didn't walk till she was almost 2 years old. Today she is a successful professional and has no physical or other limitations. Yes, we were concerned and took her to doctors, but in the end she walked when she was ready. We couldn't force it or change it. We learned something from this experience. Recognize that each stage is necessary and there to teach you something.

3. You will go through Stages 2-5 more than once during your relationship. As people grow, develop and change, so will the relationship and the business. If we go back to my garden analogy, plants go through stages of dormancy, high growth, blooming or not; it's part of nature. And external factors such as fertilizer and water and cold snaps throw plant development into a new stage. External factors can and will throw your

partnership into a new stage. Don't assume once you've reached Stage 5 and you have survived and are revitalized that you'll stay there. You'll go back through Stages 2-5 throughout the life of your partnership. It's all normal and necessary.

Points to remember:

1. The length of each stage is unpredictable.

2. You can't rush through a stage or bypass it. What you learn during each stage is invaluable.

3. Like a recipe, when you change an ingredient or amount the result is different. Such is true when you change the people in a partnership or the number of partners.

4. We never stop growing as human beings and as such our relationships will change.

5. Learning is not linear, neither are business growth and development.

6. The only constant is change. Once you accept this everything becomes easier.

7. All stages are positive and empowering if we can learn from them.

8. Nature offers us insights into what to expect relative to relationships and business.

Chapter 5
Defining Roles and Responsibilities – The First Step to Successful Partnerships

A fundamental component of success in any organization is having defined roles and responsibilities, with supporting metrics for all positions, but certainly for key or leadership positions. It is surprising how many partnerships start out without outlining who does what or even discussing roles and responsibilities. In a new partnership, each partner does everything. The goal is to get the business off the ground, generating revenues and customers. It really doesn't matter who does what; there is so much to do, and what matters is getting all the things handled. Besides, in this stage of partnership development everyone is happy and excited, and defining roles and responsibilities seems superfluous.

Here's the problem: As the business grows, so does the need to define roles and responsibilities for each partner. A business cannot grow if everyone is responsible for everything and no one is ultimately accountable for anything. If the discussion of roles and responsibilities never occurred before the partnership formed, you may be in for a big surprise and considerable disagreements. All too often multiple partners believe they have skills or strengths in specific areas and they want the role appropriate for those skills. How do you now decide, months or years into your relationship what role each partner will take on? When the roles for each partner are in dispute, how does this get settled? And how does it get handled without a lot of frustration and other emotions coming into play?

While having the roles/responsibility discussion before you join forces as partners may not eliminate problems down the road, it does ensure future conversations will be different than they would be if that discussion had never taken place. Nothing interferes with a relationship more than the element of surprise. If you and your partner are of the same mind about roles and responsibilities, that's great. If not, knowing so upfront gives you time to work through your differences before you need to create the organizational chart and outline respective roles.

Case Study: Conflict Over Roles

Two partners started a business 10 years ago. At the beginning, both partners did everything and there was no definition of roles and responsibilities. Within three years the business had grown to 20 people and it became important to define roles. The challenge was, and still is, that both partners felt they had skills in marketing and sales. While one partner took over that role, the other partner was relegated to the operational side of the house, which neither enjoys. So they often both jump into the marketing and sales area, which causes confusion for the people doing the work and friction with the other partner.

Had they taken the time to discuss roles and responsibilities when they first formed their partnership they might have avoided this situation. At the very least they wouldn't 10 years later be thrashing it out. I see no resolution to this problem now. Neither partner is willing to change his views about the roles each has and should have. And neither is willing to have the difficult conversation and come to a resolution. My guess is that for the life of this partnership this will be a topic that periodically erupts and causes friction between the partners and confusion among the staff.

Roles and Responsibilities: Creating the Plan

You are now clear that taking the time to discuss roles and responsibilities is important, but how do you begin the conversation and make the final decision? What criteria should come into the decision-making process, and how do you know when it's time to declare these roles publically?

To begin, each partner should complete the list of questions in the accompanying box on what they believe are their skills, strengths, gifts and talents. Everything should be considered and included, because as the business grows and evolves its needs will change. It's also important for each partner to recognize his or her weaknesses and outline those as well. Once you have completed this exercise for yourself, complete the list on each of your partners. I've also included a Skills and Experience exercise for you to complete. Going through these questions and exercises will help in several ways.

1. Roles can be determined by what the business needs and how each partner, based on his or her strengths and gifts, can fill that need. It puts ego on the back burner and brings the focus to the business rather than the individuals.

2. It encourages and allows for open communication that sets the stage for future discussions. If Partner A believes his strength is marketing, but Partner B disagrees and wants that role himself, this exercise is the starting point for making the decision. It takes away the "feeling" component and brings it back to what's in the best interest of the business and to helping the partnership reach its ultimate goal of finding the fork in the road.

3. As the business grows, the partnership knows in advance what each person brings to the table and what they don't. An organizational chart can be created for skills the business will need down the road. Knowing this now is all part of the planning process.

4. Knowing what to expect of one another minimizes the likelihood of judgments and assumptions arising in the future. If today you know your partner is poor at managing people but stellar at managing projects you won't become frustrated with his or her performance as a people manager. Either he or she will never hold that role or you will know what to expect and develop a work-around in advance.

5. As you consider your primary goal of building a partnership so that it will end appropriately at the point of maximum profits and satisfaction, this exercise will help you achieve this. The focus is on the business, not on the individual needs, helping to get you to that ideal point of the fork in the road as soon as possible.

CHECKLIST 5

Determine your strengths, gifts and talents.

1. What are your seven top strengths?

2. List the 10 top skills that you have used or developed in your career.

3. What unique gifts or talents do you bring? List at least five.

4. What area of responsibility have you held over the last five years? List functionally what you did, not your title.

5. What five skills do you think you are missing that are critical for the success of the organization?

6. What do you consider you areas of weakness? This is different from skills. List your top three.

CHECKLIST 6

Make an assessment of your partner.

If you have more than one, complete for each partner.

1. What do you consider your partner's top seven strengths?

2. What skills or experience does your partner have?

3. What unique gifts or talents does your partner bring?

4. What five skills do you think your partner is missing that are critical to the success of the organization?

5. What do you consider your partner's areas of weakness? List the top three.

CHECKLIST 7

Skills and Experience Exercise

1. How do you rate yourself on a scale of 1-10, with 10 being the highest in the areas of:

   ☐ Leadership

   ☐ Management

   ☐ Problem solving

   ☐ Business planning

   ☐ Business development

   ☐ Communication

   ☐ Team dynamics

   ☐ Staff development

   ☐ Planning and goal setting

   ☐ Emotional intelligence

2. How do you rate your partner(s) on a scale of 1-10, with 10 being the highest in the areas of:

   ☐ Leadership

   ☐ Management

   ☐ Problem solving

   ☐ Business planning

   ☐ Business development

   ☐ Communication

   ☐ Team dynamics

   ☐ Staff development

   ☐ Planning and goal setting

   ☐ Emotional intelligence

Criteria in the Decision-making Process

When deciding roles and responsibilities, each partner has to embrace the idea that the priority is what best serves the business. It's so easy for partners to each want to be the face of the company; after all, each is committing blood, sweat, time and probably capital. The first rule, and the one to come back to when there is disagreement, is: *What is in the best interest of the company?* What decision will we make that has the greatest positive impact on the success of the business? Take egos out of the decision. Take personal needs and desires out of the decision. Focus on the one thing that is bigger than any individual: *What will be in the best interest of the business?* What will get you to the fork in the road the quickest? I'm not suggesting this is an easy task. However, using this rule will answer the question when no other way to make the decision seems apparent.

In addition to what best serves the business, what other criteria should partners consider when deciding roles and responsibilities?

1. **What roles does the business need?** What it needs today may be different than what it needs five years from now as the business evolves. You are considering what roles are needed immediately and will likely not change over the next five years.

2. **What functional responsibilities will go under each role?** Are sales and marketing under one person or are they separate functions? Is human resources part of operations or does it stand alone?

3. **What positions have partners held in their previous companies and what were their responsibilities in those roles?** Titles don't mean much, so take the time to discuss not only the title but functionally what each partner did in those roles. This will provide insight into their skills and experience.

4. **Each partner's interests should have some influence, but only if all other factors have been considered.** If you want to be responsible for marketing but have no experience in marketing, and if someone else is more capable, then you shouldn't have this role. However, if partners have skills and experience that overlap, then individual preference should be part of the decision-making process.

5. **Your weaknesses should also be considered as part of this process.** As roles and responsibilities are outlined, consideration for one's weaknesses can help in defining the specific role. If, for example, organizational skills aren't your forte, you may need an assistant if you are chief operating officer and you have multiple areas of responsibility. This is about knowing what additional support you will need to perform your job well. It's also acknowledging where your weaknesses will have a significant impact on your success in that role.

CHECKLIST 8

Questions to ask to determine business needs.

1. What are the top five things we need to accomplish in the first year of our partnership?

2. What are the five skills you think are critical for the success of your business?

3. How do you rate yourself on these five skills?

4. How do you rate your partner(s) on these five skills?

5. What skills critical for the organization's success do neither you nor your partner possess?

6. What are the top five things you need to accomplish in years two through five?

7. What skills will be necessary for your business to reach those goals?

8. Are there others in the organization who posses these skills besides you or your partner?

9. How many people are in your organization now? What is the area of expertise for each person?

10. Where do you see each of these people functionally fitting into the organization?

11. As you look at your business in year five, how many people do you envision the organization having?

CHECKLIST 9

Business needs today and in the future.

1. Define all the roles the business needs today.

2. List the functional responsibilities under each role.

3. Define the roles you see the business needing in five years.

4. List the functional responsibilities under each role in five years.

5. List the positions each partner held previous to the partnership.

6. List the areas of responsibility each partner held previous to the partnership.

7. Create an organizational chart outlining the role/responsibility for each partner today.

8. Create an organizational chart outlining the role/responsibility for each partner in five years.

Is It Time?

Do you need to outline your respective roles and responsibilities the day you open your doors and announce to everyone what those roles are? Maybe! Customers, vendors and the like need to know which one of you they contact. Staff needs to know to whom they report. Titles sometimes matter when dealing with customers and vendors. However, what matters most is that partners understand their respective roles and responsibilities. It's not that important that the outside world believes the title of president means that one of you is in charge. You may have that title because you won the coin toss.

As the company grows in revenues and staff, people internally and externally need clear delineation of roles and responsibilities. Nothing is more confusing and ultimately detrimental to a business than having no clear lines of authority, responsibility and accountability.

Forget about finding the perfect time to communicate your organizational structure, internally or externally. Most often the issue is not when to communicate the information; it's that the partners wait till there is chaos before even beginning the discussion on defining roles. Doing so at the onset of your relationship eliminates the chaos, and the question of when to communicate becomes less important. Events take a natural course, and who owns what role becomes apparent to others.

Metrics: Critical for Evaluating Performance

As previously stated, partnerships go through stages. First, in Stage 1 comes the excitement. As the business moves into Stage 2, control becomes an issue and disagreements surface. Stages 3, 4 and 5 each stress and challenge the relationship, and the perceptions each partner has about the other changes. Expect that the relationship will change; it's typical and nothing to fret over.

Once the roles have been defined and the responsibilities agreed to, the next step is creating the performance metrics for each position. Too often this is ignored or missed altogether when partners discuss who does what. That's only natural; most of us don't like to be held to performance standards at all, let alone by our partners. After all, who are they to determine that you aren't performing your job well? The metrics discussions are further complicated if you have equal ownership, if one partner put in most or all of the capital, or there was no solid legal partnership agreement in place. Messy stuff for sure, but it is an important conversation to have.

This conversation is perhaps the most difficult one you and your partners will ever have. It requires all parties to leave their egos out of the discussions and for the emphasis to be on what's best for the business, not for the individuals. Beyond that, partners have to be willing to trust one another, accept accountability, be willing to be evaluated by one another and agree to consequences for nonperformance. This is a tall order for sure.

Ignoring the performance metrics discussion won't make the potential problems go away. The questions to be answered are:

- How are the roles and responsibilities of each partner evaluated?

- Who evaluates each partner?

- What are the consequences for nonperformance?

Tough questions, and coming to the answers is even tougher. Waiting till there is a crisis, disaster or huge mess isn't the answer. Waiting just ensures that the conversations will deteriorate to finger-pointing, judgment, accusations and strong emotions. At that point these conversations will have three elements: Emotions run strong, the stakes are high and opinions vary. Coming to agreement or even finding common ground when these components are in play is next to impossible, and legal action may be the result.

The solution is obvious: Have these conversations at the inception of your partnership and when you are outlining who does what, establishing titles and areas of responsibility. Come to agreement on performance measurements for each role. The discussions need to focus on the position or role, not the person performing that role. The performance metrics for the COO, for example, must be dictated by the needs of the business. This removes the personal element from the discussions.

How to determine performance metrics

The initial challenge with performance metrics is how to create them. Unless you have worked for a large corporation with a human resources department the likelihood is you don't know where to begin. Here is an outline of how to create performance metrics for any position.

1. **The formula:**

   • Metrics must be specific.

   • Metrics must be measurable.

   • Metrics must have a time line attached.

2. **Where to start:**

   • Define the key responsibilities of the role you hold (for example, to drive sales, to handle the finances, to create processes for…). Make a list of ALL responsibilities for this role, no matter how insignificant.

   • Pick the top 5-10 responsibilities from the list that are most critical, significant or will have the greatest impact on the business reaching the fork in the road.

   • Go through this same process with the role your partner holds and have him/her do the same for yours.

   • Compare notes and gain agreement on the top 5-10 areas or responsibility.

3. **Next:**

- Review each responsibility and make sure they are specific.

- Determine a measurement for each responsibility. Some examples are:

    a) Responsibility: to drive sales. Metric/measurement: to have 50 customers; to have 25 customers each doing $5K a year in revenue; to close a deal that is more than $10K in revenue; to have 25% of our business be repeat business from existing customers.

    b) Responsibility: to handle the finances. Metric/ measurement: to create monthly reports on receivables and expenses; to create a report on sales by customer each month; to ensure we have the most cost-effective long distance service; to take advantage of all early payment offers; all payables are up to date.

    c) Responsibility: to create a marketing campaign. Metric/measurement: to determine the six key elements of our marketing campaign; to determine costs for each of the six key elements and create a budget; to create a plan for how we are going to implement each of these elements; to create metrics to determine return on investment on each of the key elements.

Note: You will see in the above examples that the metrics are actually sub-responsibilities of larger responsibilities. "To handle sales" is really an over-arching responsibility for the person in charge of sales.

- Define a time line for each of the metrics. This is the date by when each will be accomplished. It can be two weeks or two years, but a time line is a key component to each metric.

- Revisit each responsibility and metric. Ask yourself this question: "Would someone else be able to determine specifically what is to be done and by when without interpretation by anyone?" If the answer is yes, you've done what you needed. If the answer is no or not sure, there is more work to be done.

More difficult than determining the performance metrics is deciding who evaluates the success and what are the consequences for nonperformance. We will be addressing these questions in Chapter 7 as part of the bigger discussion on decision-making.

Chapter 6
Expect Change: What's Yes Today May Be No Tomorrow

"Because things are the way they are, things will not stay the way they are." – Bertolt Brecht

Congratulations! You've had the difficult discussions on roles, responsibilities and performance metrics. You've reached agreement on all points, and the business is rocking and rolling. How long things will stay this way, no one can predict. What we can predict is that at some point one or more partners will no longer be satisfied with the arrangement, and difficult or unpleasant conversations will ensue. Feelings will erupt and partners will find themselves in conflict.

Why is the status quo no longer acceptable to one or more partners? What happened? When circumstances change, when the current state of affairs is problematic for partners, how do you manage through this and the discussions that will result?

What happened?

The first point to remember, as Henry David Thoreau said, "Things do not change; we change." In fact, it would be a sad world if people didn't grow and change throughout their lives. Sometimes those changes are caused by circumstances: an illness, a divorce, children … a variety of factors. These situations are likely to affect the needs of the individuals and thus how they think about their role. Secondly, as the business grows and changes, so will the needs and expectations of the individual partners. Adding partners changes the dynamics. Bringing on additional staff shifts the function or role of partners. Change should be expected.

Knowing the most common disputes and objections likely to crop up eliminates the "how did this happen?" question. Take a look at what issues other partnerships have faced and suggestions on how to handle each. In subsequent chapters we will be addressing some of these in more detail.

1. Dissatisfaction with role. A partner may have agreed to a role because it was what the business needed and there was no one else to fill it. But he or she was never satisfied with this role and grows increasingly dissatisfied as time goes by, making this a point of contention.

<u>**How to resolve:**</u>
- Go back to your "Business needs today and in the future" document. Evaluate whether the document still adequately depicts the business needs.

- Determine the strengths, skills and talents of the partner who is dissatisfied.

- What role might the person hold that best fits his or her skills, experience and talents different from the current role?

- If there are no options for this partner other than the current role, revisit the primary goal of the partnership – to build a partnership so it can end properly. It may require the partner who is dissatisfied to put his or her own needs aside so the business meets its objectives.

2. Role not using partner's strengths. Similar to No. 1, a partner (or partners) has taken on a role that does not use the person's strengths or gifts and talents. Perhaps the partner thought he or she was strong-armed into this role; perhaps no role used the person's strengths. It doesn't matter how or why. No one wants to have a position that doesn't use his or her strengths or provide an opportunity to do what the person does best. While they may have accepted this situation initially, sooner or later it will grate on them.

<u>**How to resolve:**</u>
- Together create a list of this partner's strengths. Come to agreement on what they are.

- Determine whether the current role can utilize the person's strengths. There may be some creative options not yet considered.

- If the current role does not best use the partner's strengths, are there other roles he or she can hold? If not, are there other responsibilities or projects the person can take on to satisfy his or her needs?

- If there are no options for this partner other than the current role, revisit the primary goal – to build the partnership so it can end properly. It may require the partner who is dissatisfied to put his or her own needs aside so the business meets its objectives.

3. Workload is too big. Whether it's perception or reality, someone believes the workload is unbalanced or the other party is not holding up his or her end. As the business grows, the workload may indeed become unbalanced. Department personnel grow from one to many, and more departments get added. These factors affect the scope of responsibility and may indeed change the workload. The second issue, not holding up his or her end of the workload, is knotty at many levels. Be aware that this subject is likely to crop up in many conversations throughout your partnership. It may take a back seat at times, but don't assume it will ever goes away.

How to resolve:

- Take a look at the organizational chart. It may be that the responsibilities of one partner have grown exponentially due to increased staff size, etc. It may be time to shift around some of the areas of responsibility held by one partner or add a senior-level person to take on some piece of the role.

- As you look at the organizational chart, assess whether there is sufficient bench strength under each partner for them to adequately handle the role. Sometimes the issue isn't too much work or too many people, but that there isn't sufficient leadership reporting to the partner so he or she is too often involved with day-to-day decisions.

- The conversation about one partner not holding up his or her end of the workload is more easily resolved if performance metrics have been developed. If they are in place, use them as a guide for the conversation. It may eliminate the perception-versus-reality dispute.

4. Difference of opinion on work/life balance. The issue of uneven workload can arise because of differences in needs and opinions about work/life balance. Family considerations, outside interests or simply energy and motivation will affect how each person defines work/life balance. As each partner's needs change, this issue will surface again and again throughout your relationship. Expect it.

How to resolve:

- Values change for us as our individual needs change. Retake the values exercise on our website and see what has changed since the last time.

- Discuss what issues, challenges or needs have changed, e.g. a partner is now taking care of an aging/ill parent or has developed health issues, etc.

- Determine what accommodations can be made by the partnership to allow the dissatisfied partner to make the changes he or she wants. Many accommodations can be handled through changes in compensation.

5. Differing views on commitment and accountability. Perceived or real lack of commitment and accountability by one or more partners sets off fireworks. This issue could be a by-product of the workload difference, but it may be a different issue altogether. When this issue surfaces, judgments and assumptions fly, and hostility and resentment are upfront and center. Expect these conversations to be unfriendly, accusatory and downright unpleasant.

How to resolve:

- If you have created performance metrics, use them to guide this conversation.

- Sometimes the metrics indicate there are no performance problems. Then determine if the issue is an individual view by one partner. For instance, one partner is frustrated with the hours another partner works. Yet if there are no issues of job performance, why does it matter? Is there some other factor such as staff perception that is important to discuss?

- If you didn't create performance metrics, you're in trouble. Step aside from the issue at hand and take the time to create performance metrics for the role. Then assess the actual performance versus the metrics. You may find there is less disconnect than you perceived.

6. Who is the face of the company? When you started the company it made sense for one person to be the face of the company. People outside the company see this person as THE decision-maker and THE key person. Partners may have agreed to take a back seat at the beginning because it made good business sense. However, the ego of anyone running a successful business will sooner or later show up, and it will no longer be acceptable to take a back seat.

<u>**How to resolve:**</u>

- Determine whether there are opportunities for all partners to be seen. Can they run more meetings, attend conferences? Think creatively, as this often resolves the challenge.

- Perception becomes reality. If a partner believes he is taking a back seat, he is. Discuss that perception. You might help him see where his perception is off.

- No partner likes to feel as if he doesn't get an equal vote or equal decision-making power. Agree to specific decisions the partner can make independently.

7. The Peter Principle emerges. It's unfortunate, but the people who helped you build the company may not be the same individuals who can help you move it to the next level. What do you do with partners who do not have the necessary skills the business needs now or to grow in the future?

How to resolve:

- This one is tough. Is there a role the person can hold in which he can still add value to the business but doesn't require him to be at the top of his game?

- Can you create special projects that become this person's responsibility? Special projects can be anything from finding resources for handling HR considerations to planning the company events (holiday parties, conferences, etc.).

- You may have to accept that this person helped you get the business to where it is today and it's like paying an annuity. Find a place where he or she can be part of the business but is not involved in the day-to-day operations.

8. Unequal ownership or balance of powers. We'll address this in Chapter 7, but suffice it to say that unequal ownership shifts the balance of power and, often, how decisions get made. A partnership of three or more creates a structure that always has the potential for dissent, disputes and voting blocks.

How to resolve:

- Unequal ownership cannot be resolved unless the partner with more is willing to give up some of his or her ownership.

- The balance of power that comes from unequal ownership is addressed in detail in Chapter 7.

9. Capital versus sweat equity. When you began, perhaps one individual put in most of the capital and others committed to sweat equity. It always happens: When there is no agreement, the one who put in the money believes he or she should make the key decisions or be the deciding vote. Those who put in sweat equity feel dismissed. It's a recipe for disaster.

How to resolve:

- Have a partnership agreement in place when you start the business. It may not eliminate the feelings, but it will handle the decision.

- If no partnership agreement is in place, it's time to address this issue. Visit an attorney and perhaps your accountant.

- Sweat equity has value. If you are the partner who has capitalized the business, don't forget you couldn't have gotten here without the other person.

- Refer to Chapter 7 for more information on handling this issue.

10. Adding partners through buy-in. If you were a sole proprietor, giving up authority to another person is difficult. Giving up power is next to impossible. Even if you are an established partnership, adding partners is a challenge. How do you make decisions on the role of the new partner? How will this addition change the roles of existing partners, the balance of powers, equity, and a host of other considerations?

How to resolve:

- If you are a sole proprietor who wants to add a partner, be aware that this partner has to be part of the decision-making process and have authority. Otherwise, he or she is an employee. Decide whether you really want a partner or simply an employee.

- Before adding a partner, determine what you are willing to give up (equity for example) and change (role considerations).

- If you are an established partnership, why do you want another partner or two or more? What skills or experience do you need that they bring? Once you know this, determining their role will be easier.

- If you are adding a partner simply to increase revenues (another attorney, accountant or other professional service area) the person still gets a vote, otherwise – again – he or she is an employee, not a partner.

11. Failure to hand over the reins. Every organization needs to build leaders in order to sustain growth. This is often a challenge in partnerships. When one or more partners want to maintain control of decision-making it is likely to cause friction with their partners and staff.

How to resolve:

- Chapter 7 addresses the decision-making question in detail.

- Partnership agreements often address this question. If you don't have one, now is the time draw one up.

- Revisit the objective of the partnership: to build it so you get to the fork in the road. Does it serve this objective to have one partner holding onto the reins?

CHECKLIST 10

Which of these factors is a point of contention in your partnership?

Check off which are causing friction in your partnership now.
Whether these are perception or reality is not the consideration.
If you are having ongoing conversations about these topics,
check them off.

☐ One or more partners dissatisfied with their role and/or area of responsibility

☐ Challenges with uneven workload

☐ One or more partners have reached their Peter Principle

☐ Work ethic questions

☐ Differing views on nonperformance

☐ Unequal ownership concerns

☐ Partner who capitalized the business no longer satisfied with arrangement

☐ No clear leadership

☐ One partner maintains primary control of decision making

☐ Other – something not on the list, add it here

Managing Through the Issues

Communication is the key to everything that works or doesn't work in your partnership. We'll be talking a lot more in upcoming chapters about the role of communication in building and maintaining a healthy partnership, but just know that communication is essential to managing through the issues on roles and responsibilities.

As stated earlier, you have to begin the conversations about roles, responsibilities and metrics at the inception of your partnership or shortly thereafter. You are destined for problems if you wait months or years until the business reaches a point where the decision can no longer be deferred. At this point the stakes are high, opinions vary and emotions get heated. This is a deadly combination for productive conversations.

Beyond having the initial conversation about roles, it's important to revisit this conversation at least annually, perhaps as part of your planning for the coming year. Things change, people change and the business changes. Regularly revisiting these topics reduces the chances of individuals' harboring feelings for years and then erupting without warning. Regular communication also demonstrates a commitment to each other and the success of the business.

Lastly, when these concerns arise, you must address them openly, honestly and frankly. Ignoring them or hoping they will go away will only make them bigger and hairier. You won't win points or positively influence the outcome by suggesting that it's the other person's problem rather than embracing it as a problem for the business. Anything short of sitting down with the other person in a meaningful conversation, with the goal of coming to a place acceptable to all parties, simply won't work.

Key points on roles and responsibilities

1. Define roles and responsibilities for each partner at the inception of the business.

2. Create appropriate metrics for each role.

3. Annually revisit the key responsibilities for each position and create new metrics as appropriate.

4. Make adjustments to roles and responsibilities as the business needs change.

Chapter 7
Power Structure and Decision-making

Nobody wants to believe his or her organization is run by a benevolent dictator or bully, and so organizations profess to collaborate on decisions, be inclusive and share ideas. However, talk is cheap and very few organizations are truly collaborative, and they can't afford to be. The reality is that when you ask people for their opinions and ideas, they assume and expect you will use them. When you don't, they become frustrated and disillusioned. Someone ultimately has to be accountable and make the decisions. Pronouncing that "the group" decided doesn't cut it with boards, especially when the results were less than stellar.

In partnerships you typically don't answer to a board, but you do answer to one another. Unlike a board of directors, whose sole interest is what's best for the business, partners see themselves intimately intertwined with the business. They are the business and often the business is their identity. Their self-interests can and often do overshadow what is best for the business or partnership, especially if that decision has negative consequences for them personally.

Yet decisions must be made. When there is equal ownership and an unequal number of partners, decisions can be made by a majority vote. That doesn't mean partners will be satisfied with the decision, but the decision-making process can be relatively clear-cut. However, the process gets murky and messy in all other partnership situations. Even if I own only 51%, does that mean by default I make all decisions?

Power structure and the decision-making process are topics that, if left unaddressed, can become constant points of contention between partners. Or they can become the elephant that sits in the corner, ignored. Remember, however, that it's not invisible just because we ignore it.

Assertive partners will do what they think needs to be done and the less-assertive will resent those decisions. And so the partners go in opposite directions that meet their own needs but not the strategic needs of the business or the partnership. A potential risk is that the partnership will end prematurely and never reach the tipping point, the fork in the road.

The solution is simple: Develop a clear decision-making process and reduce the power structure as much as is realistic. Working toward the solution isn't as simple, but success begins and ends with communication, not simply conversation.

Power Structure

Many factors contribute to an imbalanced power structure. Differences in the amount of partners' equity is certainly a biggie. Lack of legal or financial documents to support the partnership gives the more assertive partners the opportunity to take the lead. Voting blocks can form to force the outcomes of specific situations. The discrepancy between capitalization and sweat equity can lead to an imbalance of power.

Those factors are less important than the fact that imbalance exists and its cost to the organization. If you are the partner with the power, it may seem like you hold the keys to the kingdom, so to speak. Remember, however, that while it may feel good to be king, your subjects don't necessarily enjoy their status. Your partner(s) have joined you because they want to create something and be the boss, or at least have a say in decisions. They'll be resentful if they begin to feel like employees rather than equals, with limited or no decision-making capabilities. With resentment comes anger, dissention and a whole host of other emotions, all leading to a partner's ignoring the greater good and focusing on his or her own needs. It takes a lot of work to bring the partner back into the fold and rebuild trust. You spend an inordinate amount of time managing the crisis and dealing with the backlash instead of strategically developing the business. It's quite possible that you will end up changing the original decision or make concessions anyhow in order to curb the tide of resentment and its fallout. Think about this when you are playing king.

I'm not suggesting that there shouldn't be a decision-maker or that voting is an unreasonable method of decision-making. What I am suggesting is that how people feel about a power structure has a bearing on how they respond. Remember, I said earlier perception is reality. If your partners believe they are being railroaded, assume their opinion doesn't matter or are dealing with a power structure that minimizes their contributions, their actions will be governed by that belief.

Who Gets the Final Say?

I'm not being naïve here. I get that there are clearly times someone has to make a decision. The point I want to make is that it's more important <u>how</u> the decision gets made than <u>who</u> makes it. Let's assume you and a partner each own 50% of the company. How does the partnership determine who makes the decision if you aren't in agreement? Alternatively, if you own the greater percentage of the business, does that mean that you by default make the decisions, even if others disagree with you?

It's critical to discuss who makes the final decision and how decisions get made, and vital to determine the answer before you join forces as partners. At the very least this conversation should take place in Stage 1 of your relationship, while excitement and enthusiasm exists. As you enter Stage 2 and beyond, it will become increasingly difficult to have a civil conversation about this topic. It's just human nature: The more time you spend in a relationship, the more you expect to be considered.

There are numerous questions to address that will support you in deciding how decisions get made. For example: If each partner owns 50%, how is a decision made if there is a difference of opinion? Hoping one of you will back down is not the most effective process. The following questions are also available as a downloadable form on our website. Each partner should answer the questions independently. This form and the answers you each provide can be used to begin the conversation.

CHECKLIST 11

How are decisions made?

Answering these questions will start the discussion.

1. Does equity play a factor?

2. Does the partner with the most equity make all decisions, key decisions or just tie-breaker decisions?

3. What types of decisions can partners make independent of each other?

4. What types of decisions require discussion or a vote?

5. When there is a difference of opinion, how does the decision get made?

6. How is the issue of non-performance handled?

7. Who makes decisions about personal issues such as illness, time off, compensation, etc.?

You don't have to decide how you will handle every decision or situation that may arise; you just have to set up a process for handling them when they do. The decision itself is not really the big challenge. It's how the decision gets made that causes friction. I as a partner may not agree with the decision, but if I have accepted in advance the decision-making process, then I will at the very least acknowledge that the process was handled as outlined. Sometimes I will win and sometimes I will lose, which I knew in agreeing to the decision-making process in the first place.

The reality is, sometimes one partner has to make the decision and the other has to go along. There will be times when there is no clear-cut decision or there is a vote that yields no winner; then someone has to step in and take the responsibility for making the decision. Ideally, there won't be too many circumstances where you and your partner are diametrically opposed. And if you have previously decided who makes these decisions, the process is a lot smoother and generates less angst and emotion.

Chapter 8
Building a Healthy Relationship:
The Role of Communication

Underlying everything that does work and all that doesn't in our personal and professional lives is communication. In personal relationships there is an emotional bond that helps ease you through the challenges and difficulties. Business partnerships do not have the same bond. Even if you are related (see Chapter 11 on family businesses) the emphasis has to be on the business first. Remember the goal of reaching the point of maximum profitability and satisfaction so that the relationship will end well? This means the focus is on the business and what best serves the business. The relationship is there to serve the business, not the other way around.

The difficulty with communication is that it's darn complicated, and yet we don't see it as such. We believe that when we speak, we are communicating. Not so. When there is a problem with communication we don't think "Hey it's me and not him?" It's always the other guy isn't it? They weren't listening, they didn't care, they misunderstood, they were just flat wrong. This belief is what makes communication so complex and thorny.

One of my favorite quotations about communication, from Francis Garagnon, is: *"Between what I think I want to say, what I believe I'm saying, what I say, what you want to hear, what you believe you understood, and what you actually understood, there are at least nine possibilities for misunderstanding."*

There is so much truth in this quote, and it expresses the difficulty of communication. We are taught to speak, but not to communicate. As a result, we have come to collapse the concept of talking into communicating, believing they are one and the same. Communication is the cornerstone of a successful partnership. Poor, ineffective or weak communication between partners will impair the relationship, which will affect the business. You may still find the fork, but the likelihood is it will take longer or the business will never reach its full potential.

Essentials of Business Partner Communication

A wise man once told me the difference between business and day care is simply the number of years. This absolutely applies to communication between partners. I have seen partners name-calling, throwing things, walking out of the room, slamming doors and more. At times I've had to treat them like children, sending them to "time out," separating them or requiring them to apologize. I have often felt like Dr. Phil or Dr. Laura when working with partnerships. It's amazing how childish, mean and downright vindictive adults can be.

Each stage of the business and partnership development will inevitably bring about new challenges and changes in your ideas and goals. Hence, it's imperative to keep the communication channels open.

Here are Linda's rules of communication:

1. **Communicate often and regularly.** Schedule regular times with your partner. Talk about the business, concerns, challenges you are facing, competition, leadership development, succession planning ... just talk. Meeting regularly will allow you to handle little problems before they erupt into something big. And don't confuse e-mail with face-to-face communication. It won't have the same result.

2. **Don't become complacent.** It's easy to ignore the signs that problems are brewing. If you suspect there is a problem, deal with it then. Problems do not go away. They simply get uglier and more complicated as we ignore them.

3. **Set ground rules for what is inappropriate.** Is it acceptable for someone to simply walk out of the room if he or she is angry, to use four-letter words, pound on the desk or call one another names? You may laugh, but this and even worse is pretty typical behavior. One client threw a chair out of a window when he was upset. Decide what behavior and language is appropriate or not and hold one another to these standards.

4. **What information is shared?** Besides the business issues, do you want to share personal information with each another? The personal information can be a challenge. Decide what is too much and when to cut it off. When you work closely with others, the lines between business and personal can easily become blurred. Discuss what you want to share and what you don't want to know. And revisit this topic often as circumstances and needs change.

5. **Listening is more important than talking.** Listen intently and without waiting to jump in with your thoughts. If you are interrupting or waiting to share your ideas, you aren't listening. You'll learn a lot if you simply listen to what the other person is trying to communicate.

6. **Don't jump to conclusions or assumptions.** It's human nature to assume we know what someone is thinking, going to say or how he or she will react to a situation. However, once we allow our assumptions and judgments to enter into the conversations, we quit listening.

7. **Be aware of expectations.** What expectations do you have about each other regarding communication? Do you assume if there is a problem or your partner needs help he or she will let you know? How do you communicate with staff, handle challenges with customers, deal with financial issues or anything else? Are you in synch about how, when and what gets communicated to each other or staff? If not, it's time for a conversation.

8. **Don't forget agreements.** A huge challenge for partnerships is forgotten agreements. They don't have to be big; they can be commitments you made about a project or time line. Remind one another of the commitments and agreements you make and hold one another accountable. When commitments are made and there is no follow-through, trust begins to erode. Without trust, the relationship will quickly deteriorate.

9. **Revisit goals and values annually.** People's needs change. Business needs change. What was realistic when you started out may no longer be practical as the business grows or individual partners' needs change. Annually discuss your individual goals and values and what each of you wants for the business in the next three to five years. Complications are guaranteed to occur if you assume, without having a discussion, that you and your partner are in alignment about goals and values.

10. **Have a clear process to resolve conflict.** In Chapter 7 we discussed how decisions get made and the importance of a process to handle differing views or opinions. It's equally important to create a process for resolving conflict. Determining those steps before you are in the midst of a thorny situation won't eliminate the conflict. It will, however, provide a template for handling it and you'll be able to focus on the problem rather than the emotions attached to the problem. For resources on conflict resolution, visit our website.

Finkle's Rules of Engagement

1. **Remember you are adults, not children.** Children are taught not to scream, accuse, throw things, call names, stomp out the room, tattle etc. Don't be guilty of these things.

2. **Follow the golden rule.** Be respectful and treat others as you want to be treated.

3. **Time out is OK.** If emotions are high it's OK to agree to stop and come back to the discussion.

4. **Listen more than talk.** It really isn't all about you.

5. **WAIT.** This stands for Why Am I Talking? Ask yourself whether you have something significant to say or you're talking just to be heard.

6. **Keep a clean sweatsock handy.** If you can't control yourself stuff the sweatsock in your mouth.

7. **Clearly state your objective.** Whether it's a decision, to share information, ask for input etc., lack of clarity on your part will result in assumptions by the other party.

8. **Be honest, but not brutal.** Honesty is essential, brutality is not.

9. **Care more about the outcome than being right.** Who cares if you're right? All that matters is a successful outcome.

Common Ground and Joint Beliefs

Differences of opinion and conflict are going to arise in any relationship. You can't prevent them, but you can reduce the number of misunderstandings that cause conflict. Most partnerships have topics that are likely to be sources of controversy. Knowing what they are and the other person's views on these topics is a critical step in successful communication. You don't have to be in complete agreement on everything, but you have to share common beliefs about the big things.

Topics that are most likely to cause controversy within the partnership include: succession planning (to sell or not and/or an exit strategy), hiring family members (or not), how to manage, direction of the company and/or how to build the company, taking on other partners and the granddaddy of all, compensation. Once your partner has hired his son it's too late to have the discussion on hiring family members. Discovering five years into your relationship that you and your partner differ on growing the business or securing investors is like getting married and finding out five years later your spouse doesn't want children and you do. Now what? Emotions are strong, opinions vary and the stakes are high. Not an ideal scenario for rational conversations.

Compensation leads the list as the topic most likely to cause controversy. Don't think simply about salary when you discuss compensation. Compensation can include vacation time, what expenses the business pays for, what happens if someone is ill or incapacitated for six weeks and more. Waiting till your partner is going to be out of work for six weeks due to hip replacement surgery is not the best time to begin talking about whether he or she gets paid or not.

CHECKLIST 12

Controversial topics.

How many have you discussed?

☐ Hiring family members

☐ Succession plan or exit strategy for individuals

☐ Compensation

☐ Retirement options

☐ Goal of the business

☐ Growing the business – by acquisition, adding partners, investors, organically

☐ Work/life balance considerations

☐ Personal challenges such as illness, family issues etc.

☐ How will you know when you have "found the fork"

☐ Leadership style

The solution is obvious: These potentially explosive topics should be discussed at the onset of the relationship and annually thereafter. If you and your partner share the same beliefs about these matters, that's great! If not, you can discuss and come to agreement before the issues surface and become volatile. Count on views and ideas changing. An annual discussion of these topics brings them out into the open so that you can determine where you are aligned and collectively determine how to handle any differences.

Building and Maintaining Trust

Nothing destroys the fabric of a relationship more than lack of trust in the other person. Trust has two components: ethical trust and performance-based trust. Ethical trust is the honesty, principles, morals and standards that you adhere to. Performance-based trust is commitment and accountability, follow-through, admitting mistakes, basically anything that falls outside of ethical trust. When partners don't trust, whether it's ethical or performance-based, the communication will change. Building trust is only part of the equation; maintaining trust throughout the relationship helps you weather the difficult times to ensure you reach the ideal tipping point.

CHECKLIST 13

Do you trust your partner?

☐ Yes, totally.

☐ Yes, with making coffee or getting doughnuts.

☐ Only when I am carrying a gun or Taser.

☐ Never, nope, are you kidding?

It's often taken for granted that morals, ethical standards and principles are either the same or similar enough between partners that they never come up for discussion. Realistically, it's not often that partners have polar opposite views on ethics. However, views change. What one partner would consider an ethical violation in the early stages of the business may no longer be seen as such as the business changes. For example: In the beginning every customer is revered. Partners wouldn't consider cheating or being dishonest with a customer. However, as the business grows each customer is less vital. A partner may feel that little white lies don't matter or what they don't know won't hurt them. What may in the past have been considered unethical is today considered just business.

Another example: In the early years money is always a concern and every nickel counts. Partners are likely to agree on what expenses are considered business versus personal expenses. Suddenly, one partner decides that leasing his wife a car is a legitimate business expense. Is it? I doubt the IRS would say yes, but more important is what the other partners think. Do they consider this a breach of ethics?

Each of us has his or her own standards. And we can justify to ourselves any decision we make. I would never consider stealing from a company I worked for or owned. But what if my child needed an operation that was going to cost $250,000 and the insurance wouldn't pay? While I'd like to believe I would never embezzle money, I honestly can't say 100% that, given those circumstances, I wouldn't choose my child first. The point is, our own ideas of ethical behavior will change over time and circumstances may cause us to adjust our beliefs. Have the conversations about ethics at the beginning of your partnership and regularly thereafter. Nothing may have changed, but it is better to know if it has than to be caught off guard.

Inevitably, performance-based trust changes over time. Remember, in the early stages of the business the partners have shared their visions for where they want to go and how they are going to get there. Each partner is doing whatever it takes to build the business and make it successful. The issues of commitment, accountability, individual performance or blame simply don't come up. Once the business has reached Stage 3, partners' views may change. One may no longer be willing to put in the same time and effort as they had previously. A partner may become dissatisfied with another's job performance. Standards and expectations change, and thus performance becomes an issue. Mistrust begins when you're unable to count on your partner, and sets in motion the question of performance-based trust issues.

Most of us simply trust others. We believe them and have faith in them until they prove unworthy. Once trust is broken it's difficult, though not impossible, to regain. It requires all parties to be willing to set aside past beliefs and perceived injustices. It's more than just giving the other person a chance. It means a willingness to again believe in and depend on the person. For most, this is a tall order; for many, it's unobtainable.

Communication is the key to building and maintaining trust, and having performance metrics is the key to communication. It will provide a starting point for the conversation. It may not make the conversation easier or less emotionally charged, but it moves the conversation away from "I think," "you did," "you didn't" and "I believe" and brings it back to the agreed-upon business metrics. With regular communication you will learn where you think differently and where you are aligned. Surprises are less likely to occur.

It all sounds so simple. Just talk regularly, share information and all will be right with the world and your relationship. While not communicating regularly is a recipe for problems, there is no guarantee that frequent communication will eliminate them. Several criteria must exist for conversations to be productive and effective. Each is a factor in building and maintaining trust. Omitting one may not be disastrous, but ignoring several is certain to cause the conversations to go poorly.

Make space for differences. One of the wonderful things about human beings is that we are different from one another. How we think, analyze, adjust, change, grow, handle problems makes us each unique. Making the space for those differences is fundamental to unguarded communication.

Be willing to admit mistakes. We all make mistakes. Perfection is not a state to aspire to, it's a process. Be willing to admit your mistakes, how you handled them and what you learned. Trust builds when others know you'll step up and accept responsibility for your mistakes.

Ask for help. Asking for help reveals a great deal about you. Only an individual with a high level of confidence in themselves can feel comfortable asking for help. It lets others adjust their expectations. It also prevents the guessing game or assumptions. Others know they can count on you to tell them when you need help so they don't have to guess whether things are going well or make any assumptions. Guessing and assumptions do not bode well for building trust and successful communication.

Commitment, accountability and follow through. If you commit to something, follow-through and accountability must be part of the equation. Without follow-through and/or accountability, others don't know what to expect and trust is broken. And offering excuses when you don't follow through doesn't cut it. It demonstrates a lack of accountability on your part. Fundamental to performance-based trust is follow-through and accountability.

Set aside judgment and blame. When things go wrong it's natural to want to look for someone to blame. Judgment precedes blame. Think about it. We don't blame if we haven't already prejudged. Once we go to blame, the other party's defenses come up and communication ends, even if the conversation continues. When we close the communication channels, trust cannot survive.

Include emotional intelligence. Some of us are born with a greater emotional intelligence quotient than others. But emotional intelligence is a skill that can be learned through practice. Using emotional intelligence in your communications means by default you are listening to the other person. When people feel heard it builds trust.

Feel compassion and gratitude. Compassion and gratitude need to be part of conversations if trust is to be realized. It's so easy to look at what's wrong, what's not working or what's left to do. Take time to include gratitude in your conversations and compassion for yourself and your partner.

Have the difficult conversations. The biggest obstacle to maintaining trust is ignoring the difficult conversations. Many people are conflict-averse. They perceive these difficult conversations as conflict and thus avoid them. But ignoring or avoiding them doesn't make them go away. Over time they get bigger and more difficult to deal with. If you want to build and maintain a high-trust relationship you have to be willing to have those difficult conversations you'd rather sidestep.

Trust starts with communication. However, even if you are communicating regularly, you can lose trust in your partner. I'm not suggesting that frequent conversations are a guarantee for building a high-trust relationship. What I do know is that not communicating, not having the difficult conversations or poorly handling the conversations you do have will eventually erode any trust that existed. When this happens the relationship will change, perhaps irrevocably. And that will have a detrimental impact on the partnership reaching its primary goal of ending the partnership successfully. Sure, you can still reach the goal, but the personal toll it takes on the partners and even staff will be enormous. And you will struggle to get to the goal as quickly as realistically possible. Trust or the lack thereof has a huge effect on how and when you reach your partnership goal.

CHECKLIST 14

Factors in building trust.

How many exist in your partnership?

☐ Avoid blame and judgment

☐ Feel commitment and accountability

☐ Accept responsibility for mistakes

☐ Allow for differences

☐ Don't avoid the difficult conversation

☐ Expectations clearly communicated

☐ Ethical standards agreed upon

Living with Differences

Here's the reality: When problems surface with your partner, you have a finite number of options. You can ignore them (not a good idea), you can duke it out, discuss and come to agreement or compromise, or dissolve the partnership. Even discussing and coming to an agreement or compromise may leave one of you feeling dissatisfied. There is no perfect solution, but doesn't mean you should accept doing nothing.

Complications are going to exist in any relationship. Constant fighting, however, should not. When problems arise, views differ or challenges exist, the answer does not need to be combative behavior. Aside from the fact that endless bickering and snipping at each other solves nothing, it also creates frustration for one another as well as the staff. It negatively impacts decision making, staff satisfaction and turnover, customer relations and the long-term success of the business.

Sometimes we simply have to live with the differences. I'm not suggesting you merely shut up. That's not healthy for you, the relationship or the business. I am saying that everything doesn't have to turn into World War III. You have to determine which issues are important enough to discuss and resolve. It may be best to live with and overlook some that are simply annoying. If your partner shows up late for staff meetings, it may be important to discuss how employees perceive this. On the other hand, if your partner shows up for work at 10 a.m. and you wish he were there at 8:30, is it important enough to argue about? I don't have the answer. What I'm saying is that how you feel about it shouldn't be the reason to discuss or not. The consideration should be how important it is in the grand scheme of things and what is the effect on you and your company reaching its goals? Living with differences is important to building a healthy relationship.

Chapter 9
Building Your
Partnership Culture

"Culture is a little like dropping an Alka-Seltzer into a glass – you don't see it, but somehow it does something."
– Hans Magnus Enzensberger

Corporate culture is what makes companies unique. It also has a bearing on hiring, retention, leadership development, creativity, ethics and standards, customer loyalty, decision-making and the ability to adapt, to name just a few. There's clearly no doubt that company culture is a topic worth discussing. There are hundreds of articles and books on company culture. They advise you on the importance of defining your corporate culture and provide examples of various types.

Is corporate or company culture synonymous with partnership culture? In absolute terms, the partnership is a company or corporation, so from this perspective the two terms can be viewed as interchangeable. However, partnerships are a unique type of company. There is no other corporate structure where two or more individuals operate the company as co-owners with all the privileges and risks this entails. Partners each have decision-making and voting privileges, and their compensation is often determined by not only their individual performance but also by the overall success and profitability of the business. In general, non-partnership businesses determine salary by grade level utilizing generally accepted fair market value for a position. Performance may enter into salary considerations, but employees do not expect their compensation to be tied to the profits of the company. These considerations make the partnership culture unique.

Another difference is that a partnership has not only a partnership culture but also a subculture, which is the corporate culture. Typically the company culture that exists within a partnership is directly correlated to the partnership culture. In most companies, the CEO defines the corporate culture, which is associated with that one individual's views and vision. In partnerships, a group of two or more defines first the members' relationship and all the elements associated with that relationship, which defines the partnership culture. Out of that relationship the company culture gets defined, explicitly or tacitly.

There is no other type of organization in which the culture is so clearly defined by a group of individuals, often with different and self-serving needs as a partnership. The admission or departure of partners will affect the interactions between partners and, consequently, the group dynamics. The same is true as the average age of the partners change. The needs, values and vision that partners in the 55+ age group will often be very different from that of the partners in the 35-50 age group. If the partnership becomes mostly Young Turks, expect new topics to come up and the potential for many things to change. When the members of the partnership change the dynamics change and you should assume the partnership culture will also change.

Defining Your Culture

Corporate culture is the sum of the values, customs, traditions and beliefs that make a company unique. Basically it's how you, your partners and your staff interpret experiences and behave, individually and in a group. These values, beliefs and interpretation of experiences influence ethical standards and management behavior. With a partnership you will need to define both the partnership culture and the company subculture. It doesn't matter how you characterize the culture or what labels you attach to the definition. The culture lets others know your values, beliefs and what to expect. It provides the framework for decision-making and behaviors. Basically the culture is the tenets by which you, your partners and the company exist. It controls the way you interact with one another and with stakeholders outside the company.

How do you begin to define your culture? Let's take a look at the partnership culture before drilling down into the company culture. There are dozens of factors to consider. Is every partner expected to be involved with business development or generate revenue? Does each partner have an equal voice in decisions unrelated to their percentage of ownership? Are there expectations related to hours worked, administrative details and acceptable behaviors? Are terms like "vacation" and "sick leave" loosely or explicitly defined? Is there general agreement on the direction of the company and management style? Do partners want to work through differences and challenges or divide and conquer? Does one partner have ultimate decision-making authority? The list of topics to consider can be enormous, or it can be minute. It will all depend on what the individual partners determine is part of their belief system.

CHECKLIST 15

Defining your partnership culture.

1. **Egalitarian:** We are all equal

2. **Authoritarian:** One of us is king, everyone else is here to serve

3. **Democratic:** As long as everyone agrees

4. **Inconsistent Leadership:** Do as I say, not as I do

5. **Anarchy:** Revolution precedes change

6. **Laissez-faire:** We make it up as we go along

7. **Collaborative:** Everyone has a say

8. **Pragmatic:** It is what it is

9. **Idealistic:** It will all be perfect

10. **Three Musketeers:** All for one and one for all

11. **Culture:** What's that

The next step is to define your corporate culture. Are you a company that leads or follows? Is creativity and forthright communication encouraged? Are metrics identified and adhered to? Is staff encouraged to take risks and make decisions or is there a supreme being who makes all final decisions? You get the idea.

Once you have defined your culture, don't keep it a secret. It's essential to know who you are as a company (your culture) and communicate this information to others inside and outside your business. It can help build loyalty, attract customers and employees and distinguish you from competitors. At the very least it will help people both inside and outside understand expectations and provide the guidelines they need for decision-making.

Partnership Culture and the Impact on the Business

The partnership culture and the company culture are intertwined and thus what affects one will affect the other. As I previously stated, you can expect the partnership culture to change over time, thanks to external forces and changing priorities. It's inevitable. Therefore, as the partnership culture changes, so will the company culture.

The partnership culture will define the corporate culture. For example, if you have determined that the partnership culture includes a family orientation, then this is likely to carry over into the corporate culture. A partnership culture that includes an expectation of business development activities for each partner will influence management behavior and maybe how definitively processes, standards and procedures are defined. Consider issues such as identity, communication problems, human resources problems, ego clashes, and intergroup conflicts, which all fall under the category of partnership differences. There is no getting around the fact that the culture that is created by the partnership is intertwined with how the business is run. If there is something about the way the business is operating that causes you heartburn, first look at the partnership culture. The likelihood is the issue begins there.

CHECKLIST 16

Rules to make your partnership culture work:

1. Everyone is equal and deserves to be heard.

2. Share your toys, this playground is meant for everyone.

3. Don't be a bully.

4. Play fair: Ignore the adage "all's fair in love and war."

5. Focus on winning the game, not the battles.

6. Remember this is about business, not friendships.

7. Don't change the rules without telling the rest of the team.

8. Show up and suit up.

9. Practice makes perfect. If at first you don't succeed, try, try again.

10. Remember the goal: to build the partnership so that it reaches the maximum point of profitability and satisfaction for all, allowing it to end properly.

A final comment. By now I hope you are recognizing a couple of themes. Relationships change; the business changes; priorities, needs and values change and it's all to be expected. Acknowledging this will prevent the "why is this happening?" syndrome. Second, the cornerstone to everything that works and everything that doesn't work in the partnership is communication. Having regular and meaningful conversations about key issues, addressing the difficult conversations and coming to agreement are the foundations of sound communication. Lastly, take the time to discuss, define, decide, determine and, yes, even disagree. These are true for building your partnership and your partnership culture. All they take is time and a profound willingness to invest in your partners and the business.

Chapter 10
The Compensation

"When I was young I thought that money was the most important
thing in life; now that I am old I know that it is."
— Oscar Wilde

Oscar Wilde's quote epitomizes how most people think about money. Money not only buys you the necessities of life, it provides status, a sense of confidence and of course the opportunity to live a life you want.

Money means different things to different people, but for most people in the workforce compensation is an issue, whether you are in a partnership or not. Everyone wants to be compensated fairly and appropriately. Of course what is deemed fair and appropriate is the big question. Consider this. How often do you hear your friends and colleagues tell you they are satisfied with their compensation package? I suspect not often. Even if they are satisfied with their salary, they are grumbling about benefits or wondering whether a colleague, who in their opinion doesn't perform as well as they do, is paid more.

In companies other than partnerships you may have some input into your salary, but you have no voting rights or decision-making capabilities. And rarely if ever do you have a say on other parts of your compensation. Now, consider what it's like to be a partner in a company. One of the advantages is that you can vote on the outcome of compensation decisions and how these decisions get made.

Some partnership agreements will address compensation, loosely or explicitly. While not every aspect of compensation will be addressed, some things can be spelled out. If you have yet to establish a partnership, then speak with your attorney about compensation and what is reasonable to include in the partnership agreement.

Compensation leads the list of partnerships' challenges. The question of money is always on the table or at least on the minds of the partners. After job performance, it is the single biggest issue that triggers disagreements, frustration and, at times, knock-down, drag-out fights. It is a constant threat to the stability of the partnership and the business.

Compensation Challenges

The fact that multiple people believe they have a right to decide on this topic is just one challenge partnerships face related to compensation. Another is that the topic of compensation is broad and has so many facets. If salary were the only consideration there would still be disagreements, but the decisions would be manageable. However, compensation discussions go beyond salary, benefits and retirement options. And so the discussions are thorny, complicated, and messy and you should expect emotions to run high.

Let's examine at some of the challenges partnerships face regarding compensation.

1. **Salary – how is it decided?** At the beginning, partners are often willing to forego huge salaries while the business is in the building phase. However whether it's discussed or not, they expect that as the business grows, so will their salary. The bone of contention between partners often is the timing and the amount of salary increases. How do these decisions get made? Is it based on the personal needs and desires of the partners or what's in the best interest of the business? Are the two mutually exclusive? Isn't what's best for the partners best for the business? If a partner feels strapped financially can he or can she put forth their best effort? Is there an across-the-board increase for all partners at the same time? The list of questions on salary can go on and on.

   There is no right or wrong way to answer the salary question. The partnerships I work with have many different ways to handle salary and salary increases. I would suggest that when there are only a few partners, don't let the individual needs of one partner dictate either the decision or how the decision gets made. The business and the partnership cannot be responsible for the individual choices one partner and/or his family makes. If his salary is putting a financial strain on him, then he must make a choice. He can identify ways to drive more revenue to the business, find ways to increase profitability or reduce his own personal expenses. Or he may have to choose to question whether this partnership fits his and his family's needs and lifestyle. Salary considerations have to be right for the business first and for individual needs second.

2. **Pay for performance or not.** What measurement does the partnership use to determine how to compensate? Is the rainmaker automatically compensated differently than the others? Are metrics for each job determined, performance evaluated against those metrics and then compensation paid in direct correlation to performance? What happens to a partner's income when his or her performance drops below the acceptable level? What happens if it exceeds the performance expectations?

As with all salary considerations, there is not a right way to decide whether to pay for performance. The question itself brings forth dozens of other questions and considerations. How they are answered will, without a doubt, cause disagreement and dissent. If there are just two of you, then possibly the question of pay for performance does not need to be addressed; only you two can make that determination. As the number of partners increase, however, you should expect this topic to arise, especially if there is a significant rainmaker amongst you or a serious question about one or more partners' job performance.

3. **Unequal ownership – does this mean unequal compensation?** How the ownership of the company was determined is not a consideration for this discussion. All that is important is to answer this: Does the percentage you own directly correlate to compensation?

4. **What benefits are included in the compensation package?** Federal and state laws may dictate what has to be included for all partners if it's included for one. Consult your attorney or human resources professional for details to be sure you are in compliance. This means the broad brushstrokes. Do

all partners have a company car? Does the company pay for expenses related to automobiles even if the company does not own the cars? What costs are covered by the company and what is the individual partner expected to cover?

Are partners allowed to take as much sick leave, vacation and personal time as they want or are specific amounts allocated? Can the company accountant (or bookkeeper) be used to pay personal bills for each partner? Can the administrative staff handle personal business for the partners such as errands, booking vacations, ordering gifts or whatever?

Such issues typically bubble up because of abuse by a partner. Expect that sooner or later, whether you are a partnership of 2, 22 or 222, these issues will come to the table and need to be addressed.

5. **What expenses are included?** This is often a sticky area. What constitutes a legitimate business expense and what becomes a personal expense? Any time a partner uses an asset for both business and personal purposes (car, cell phones, computer, BlackBerry etc.), are all costs absorbed by the business or are some allocated to personal use?

   Then there are meals, hotels and travel. Is the business going to pay for accommodations at a four-star hotel or a first-class upgrade for air travel? What might not seem that important today may, over time, erupt into heated disagreements. Without a doubt, if you are the partner who is running the operations while your partner is the face of the company and traveling frequently, sooner or later the discussion on expenses will surface.

6. Can a partner take a spouse or significant other on business trips and have the business cover these expenses? I've known partners who took their spouses and children on trips and expected the business to pay for them. Inequity becomes a problem. What if you have two children and your partner has four? What if you have no spouse or SO? Again, this doesn't come up at the beginning of the partnership, when usually there isn't enough money to consider covering expenses for family members. But such issues are likely to surface as the business becomes more successful and individual partners look for ways to increase their compensation without it being taxable.

Which expenses are covered by the business can significantly change individual compensation. As with salary, there is always the question about equality. Does the percentage of ownership relate to what is covered as an expense or are all partners treated equally, unrelated to their ownership percentage?

7. **Retirement – the big question.** Sooner or later one or more partners will want to retire. They may determine a point when they will no longer be working or want to consider a step-down approach to reducing their hours over several years. How does the company handle compensation for a retiring partner? This is a big issue, and questions regarding salary, benefits, expenses and ownership retention need to be addressed and answered.

8. **Bonuses.** This is not unlike the discussion on salary and the pay-for-performance question. If you can address those two challenges, you'll have the template for how to address the issue of bonuses.

9. **The annuity – compensating for sweat equity.** It's not uncommon for one partner to put up most or all of the equity to start the business while the other contributes sweat equity. The partnership agreement may already address the issue of compensation and how it relates to the partner's percentage of ownership. However, sooner or later the partner who puts up the money is going to feel his or her compensation should not be equal to others. I've seen this occur dozens of times. Should the business equally compensate partners who invested money versus those who invested sweat equity?

10. **To sell or not, and how does this affect compensation.** At some point you may want to sell either the business or just your ownership. Find someone who specializes in assessing company value before you begin the compensation discussions. These discussions will differ depending on whether you are selling the company or whether you are selling your ownership percentage to the other partners. Any number of factors come into consideration – percentage of ownership, partnership agreement (assuming you have a legal document in place), the needs and desires of other partners and the assessed value of the company, just to name a few. The same is true if you want to buy out your partner. How is a partner compensated for his or her ownership, and contribution to the success of the business and what expenses are covered by the business and for how long?

CHECKLIST 17

Compensation Questions:

Answer yes or no to each of these questions and then compare notes with your partner.

YES NO

☐ ☐ Do you think compensation should be based on individual performance by each partner?

☐ ☐ Should all partners be compensated equally?

☐ ☐ Do you agree that a partner who drives revenue should be compensated differently from others?

☐ ☐ Would you say the amount of equity a partner has should affect his or her compensation?

☐ ☐ Do you believe all partners should earn the same salary even if other components of their compensation are different?

☐ ☐ Are bonuses paid based on the profitability of the company?

☐ ☐ Should partners agree on travel expense considerations such as hotel rates, air fair, etc.?

☐ ☐ Is it acceptable for a partner who travels frequently to use his mileage to upgrade to first class?

☐ ☐ If the business uses a credit card with an awards program, are the points to be used by the business even if the card is in the individual partner's name?

☐ ☐ Should there be a limit on how much a partner receives for expenses such as a car or car allowance, telephone, computer and other equipment he or she uses?

☐ ☐ Do you believe in unlimited vacation, sick leave and time off for partners?

☐ ☐ Should salary be determined by the needs of the partners and not necessarily tied to the profitability of the business?

☐ ☐ Should gifts, awards, reward trips or conferences be equally distributed between partners?

☐ ☐ May partners reduce their work hours at any time as long as their compensation is adjusted accordingly?

☐ ☐ Should a partner who capitalized the business be paid more than a partner who put in sweat equity?

Compensation is a big, thorny, difficult subject that gets more complex the longer you are in business, the more successful the business and the more partners you have. The likelihood that all partners will be satisfied with all decisions is nil. Additionally, unless the company is just you and a partner, you have the well-being of other people to consider besides that of the partners'. There is nothing that frustrates employees more than feeling as if the partners are raking in the money, giving it all to themselves and not adequately compensating their workers. If your employees are not treated fairly their performance will suffer and/or they won't be around for long. Performance and morale issues as well as turnover are costly to your business.

Remember the primary purpose for building the partnership was to find the fork in the road, that point where the business has reached maximum profitability and satisfaction for a partner (or partners). The intended outcome is always to build the partnership in a manner that will allow it to end properly. The end does not mean the business dissolves. It could mean retirement for a partner, sale of the business to other partners or a merger or acquisition. The intention was never to have the partnership exist forever in the way it began. What's best for the partners may not be in the best interest of the business. This makes the compensation issue so complicated.

A final note. While partnerships are two or more individuals who operate the company as co-owners, there needs to be a mechanism in place for how decisions get made when partners don't agree. In Chapter 7 we covered power structure and decision-making and offered ideas and solutions to this problem.

Chapter 11
Family Businesses

Relationships, whether personal or professional, are a challenge. To work, they require a significant investment in the relationship and in the people involved. In personal relationships, we have an emotional investment in the other person. This emotional attachment often creates a safe place for difficult conversations and dealing with challenges. Business relationships don't have the emotional component, nor should they. I discussed in Chapter 8 the role of communication for the success of the business. Go back and read it again before reading this chapter. Communication plays a critical role in the success of any business and with partnerships even more so.

Family businesses are a unique type of partnership. They have both the personal relationship with the emotional attachments and the business component. In addition, they bring all the drama, history and dysfunctional aspects of families to the business. And they bring other family members (spouses, parents and maybe even children) to the relationship and the business even if they aren't involved in running the business. There is a different set of expectations with family partnerships and these expectations are part of what makes family businesses unique.

What's Unique About Family Partnerships?

First, that they are families. Families are analogous to an ecosystem. They are complex sets of relationships that function independently of one another but are dependent on one another at the same time. Like an environmental ecosystem, if one part is damaged it has a negative effect on everything else. Divorce, separation, health or financial problems create challenges not just for the family members but also for the partnership and the business.

Second, family members come to the relationship, and the business, with a well-formed set of ideas, assumptions and beliefs about other family members. They've had years of history together, witnessed one another's behaviors and observed how other family members interact with them. Because of this history and the assumptions, beliefs and judgments that exist, communication is a huge challenge. Family members have spent years developing their own way of communicating. It often doesn't blend well with the communication necessary to run a successful business.

Third, family partnerships often must accept family members who aren't qualified or lack the skills or abilities required to perform the duties of the position or to be an asset to the business. No other partnership or business would be as accepting of this type of situation. Furthermore, they are willing to accept non-performance and do nothing about it. In very few situations are family businesses willing to terminate a family member. Thus, others carry family members, even when it's a poor business decision.

Fourth, family partnerships are dealing with three entities, the partnership, the family and the business. No other partnership has the additional dimension of the family. Determining what is good for the partnership and what best serves the business is difficult enough. At times they may actually be in direct conflict. What serves the business may not serve the family. Trying to add in what is also best for the family is a herculean task.

Fifth, role and responsibility confusion is more pronounced in family partnerships than other types of partnerships. This is partially true because the family business often accepts poor or non-performance from family members. One family member may be a figurehead while someone else actually does all the work. Frequently, parents or grandparents resist causing friction between siblings or cousins, so they skate around the issue of clearly defined roles and responsibilities.

Lastly, family partnerships have an expectation of longevity and lifetime commitment. Members of the business assume the partner- ship will continue and the only changes will be which family members join or leave the business. It means that for family partnerships, not only is finding the fork more difficult, it may be impossible for them to consider this as an option. Thus, if their ultimate goal is to pass the business from one generation to the next rather than the goal of building the business so it can end properly, their decision-making process will be different from other partnerships'. This is not to say family partnerships can't be successful, many obviously are. However, with the focus on business continuation to provide employment to family members they may overlook factors that ensure business success and profitability.

Unique Characteristics of Family Partnerships

1. The business is negatively impacted by family situations (divorce, illness, death, etc.).

2. Roles and responsibilities are often ill-defined.

3. Non-performance by a family member or lack of skills or ability is accepted and tolerated.

4. Family dynamics and history come into play.

5. Extended family becomes part of the equation. The spouse, children and parents are in the relationship.

6. The partnership includes the partners, the business and the family. This adds an extra dimension.

7. Business continuation is the focus.

Can You Be a Family and Run a Business Together?

Thousands of families are already running businesses together. The question is not simply, can you be a family and run a business together. The real question is, can you run a family business, have it be successful, build a business with an eye toward ending it properly (finding the fork in the road) and have the family still enjoy being a family? Does the family business interfere with the family dynamics and/or do the family dynamics interfere with the business? The obvious answer to both is yes. How could they not? As stated above, families are a type of ecosystem, and what affects one part of the ecosystem impacts other parts.

But yes, you can have a family partnership, have it be successful and still have a family that likes one another and wants to spend time together. However, family members will have to address the unique challenges that a family business faces. Ignoring them will not only lead to the poorhouse, it is likely to cause irreparable tears in family relationships and perhaps the family unit as well.

You might not, however, be able to have a family partnership that focuses on finding that point of maximum profitability and satisfaction so it ends properly. In order to do so, family members have to agree on a goal that may be counter to their individual needs. That is difficult enough for individuals; for families, it may be unachievable.

Challenges Facing Family Partnerships

Every partnership has a unique set of challenges and problems. Many of the challenges that exist in other partnerships are exaggerated in a family business. Family businesses go through various stages of growth and development, just like any other business. Some of the challenges are more evident once the second and subsequent generations enter the business. Regardless of when the problems rear up, they can't be ignored or swept under the carpet. We've already discussed how problems don't go away because we ignore them. They simply get bigger and more difficult to deal with. In a family partnership, the problems not only affect the business and the partnership, they affect the family and the family relationships.

Knowing the challenges that family partnerships face won't eliminate them. It also doesn't mean they won't reoccur. However, as in other partnerships, if you are aware of what to expect you can adopt both preventive and prescriptive approaches to managing these challenges.

1. **Informality.** Particularly evident in family businesses is an absence of clear policies and business norms for family members. Individual family members might not even participate in the day-to-day running of the business. These situations make it difficult to control family members.

2. **Tunnel vision.** Family businesses tend to look to family members for opinions, ideas and how to operate the business. This leads to seeing and doing things the same old way, lack of diversity and often an inability to adapt to outside changes.

3. **Paternalism.** Control is often centralized. This leads to tunnel vision and an inability to let new ideas bubble up and be considered. Sooner or later the only people in key leadership positions are family members.

4. **High turnover of non-family members.** Any employee who is looking for career advancement will seek another job when they feel that a family member will always advance over an outsider regardless of performance. And it is frustrating to employees to realize management may be incompetent but nothing will be done about it because it's a family member.

5. **Compensation.** Go back and reread Chapter 10. Then think about how this plays out in the family partnership and you'll realize you are in a snake pit. All family members in the business regardless of their role, responsibility or their individual performance feel entitled to a compensation package on par with other family members.

6. **Ownership, power struggles and decision-making.** These challenges are more pronounced in a family partnership. In any other type of partnership you may not agree with the decision-making process or the result, but you are likely to accept it because you understand how it benefits the business. Families just think differently. And since family dynamics are ever-present, they will be front and center during these times.

7. **Communication problems are rampant.** Families have learned to communicate in a certain way. Triangulation is fairly common in family communication. That is, one family member will not communicate directly with another member, but will communicate with a third, forcing the third family member to then be part of the triangle. Just imagine the challenges this can cause for the partnership and the business.

8. **Performance problems.** Nobody likes to fire. Now, imagine having to fire your brother/sister, son/ daughter, cousin or your mother/father because of repeated performance problems. Won't happen. I'm not saying it never happens. I've worked with businesses where it did. But it didn't happen quickly, and in many cases they simply can't pull the trigger and make it happen at all.

9. **Acceptance of personal issues.** It can be a divorce, health, substance abuse problem or something else that affects the business, but a family partnership will tolerate things with one another that they would never tolerate with a non-family member.

10. **Non-direct family lineage in the business.** It can be a step-child or a spouse of one of the children or some other scenario. Someone outside the direct lineage comes into the business. Any number of challenges can emerge as a result.

11. **Mom and Dad still playing a role.** Sometimes it is useful to the company and family members for parents to continue an active role in the business. However, when older family members try to preserve status quo and resist change, the business stagnates and family feuds erupt.

Seven Keys to a Successful Family Partnership

1. PHILOSOPHY: Identify core values, vision and goals

2. COMMITMENT: Following strong leadership

3. STRATEGY: Knowing the cost-benefits balance

4. HARMONY: Resolving family disputes

5. COMMUNICATON: Building a constructive communication strategy

6. COLLABORATION: Managing division of labor and delegation of responsibilities

7. DECISION MAKING: Willing to make the decisions that best serve the business

An entire book could be written on family partnerships: what makes them unique; their trials and tribulations; and how to build a successful family business. I've included this chapter not to address all those considerations, but simply to demonstrate that a family business is a unique entity. They face all the same challenges as other partnerships, and more. The approach to running and building a family partnership has to take into account the additional element of the family. As I stated in the beginning of this chapter, family partnerships have the personal relationships, with all their emotional attachments and dynamics, along with the business component. No other partnership has this inherent dynamic. It's why I felt family partnerships deserved an entire chapter.

Chapter 12
Special Situations
or Challenges

We've already established that partnerships are unique and face situations and challenges that no other type of business encounters. With this in mind, I have grouped these challenges and special situations into categories. We've covered a lot of ground thus far. There are, however, some situations or challenges that did not fit neatly into the previous categories. I have included them in this chapter.

CHECKLIST 18

Special Situations:

How many apply to you?

- ☐ Everyone wants to be equal

- ☐ Founder only thinks he wants partners

- ☐ Partner no longer satisfied with role but no others are available

- ☐ Buy-in to partnership

- ☐ Medical practices include being on-call

- ☐ Partner reaches Peter Principle

- ☐ Everyone agrees to what is considered fair and commits to this

- ☐ Founder unable to give up control

- ☐ Partners treated as employees not equals

- ☐ Changing roles and difficulty adjusting to the change

1. **The founder – to partner or not.** Any entrepreneur can reach a point where he believes his business growth and/or income is capped. The next step might be to bring on partners to help him expand and capitalize the business, and provide expertise he doesn't have. The expected outcome is to improve business profits and the income of the founder.

   The challenge is not in identifying partners, determining compensation formulas or even coming to terms that will be addressed in a legal document. The core issue, the question the founder has to answer, is to determine whether he or she really wants partners, as opposed to employees. People who are entrepreneurs by nature have a high level of confidence in themselves and usually a need to control. Being an entrepreneur who gets to make all the decisions is different from being an entrepreneur who has partners. It's not uncommon for a founder to take on partners and still want to maintain control of all decisions. Someone who doesn't want to give up or share control should look for employees, not partners.

2. **Buy-in has to be fair.** If you determine you want to bring in other partners, the buy-in has to be fair. They can't be a giveaway to a new partner. Nor can they be so onerous that the new partner is essentially denied equal compensation forever because of his need to pay off this huge debt over years.

3. **Partner reaches their Peter Principle.** It's a hard reality of life, but often the person who helped get the business to its current level of success may not be the one who can get the business to the next step and beyond. It's not uncommon for a partnership to encounter a situation where a partner has

reached his or her Peter Principle or skill level. Now what? What are you options? Regardless of how the situation is handled, you can expect this to be unpleasant, nasty and possibly result in litigation.

4. **A partner determines his or her role is not satisfying.** I've said it over and over. People's needs change and the needs of the business change. It's fairly typical for a partner to decide that the current position or role she holds is no longer satisfying her. What do you do if there is no other role for her within the company? You can't expect her to suffer in silence, or at least not for long. You should anticipate this scenario presenting itself as the business grows. It happens all the time.

5. **Changing role of founder.** We've already discussed that the partnership will change as the business goes through the developmental stages. Roles and responsibilities of the partners will change accordingly. Assuming there was a founder who then decided to add partners, what we didn't discuss was the changing role of the founder. This is different from No. 1 above. This challenge is the recognition by the founder that over time his role will need to change, which is a difficult transition for many.

They don't know when to make the transition, what that transition means to them (what will they do now?) and how to get comfortable with the reality that they will not be involved with many (or most) decisions. Their role is no longer to run the business, but to set strategy, to build relationships and to help create the vision. It's tough for most founders to move from operational to tactical and feel comfortable letting go of the reins.

6. **Everyone wants to be an equal partner.** This will happen at some point; people will want compensation for an equal amount of work done, equal say in making decisions and so forth. Let's face it, no matter what your title, if you don't have an equal voice, you are an employee. If you wait to address the question of equality until the issue occurs or is about to occur, then it becomes personal and a lot harder to deal with. Without a doubt it will cause lots of hard feelings. Determine how you will address this at the beginning or your partnership, when it's a business decision and not personal. Nevertheless, in my opinion, it is absurd to expect someone to be a partner and not be equal.

7. **Commitment to fairness.** Fairness to everyone is the most important element of a successful partnership and often a challenge. If everyone is treated fairly, the problem people will still complain, but won't get a lot of traction. How a partnership accomplishes fair treatment for everyone begins with all partners being committed to fairness. Of course the difficulty is in getting everyone to agree as to what's fair.

8. **Medical practices are unique.** Medical practices are unique because of the on-call issue. It's always a point of contention as to when someone can opt out of night/weekend on-call, how long the person can do so before he or she has to retire and what the financial penalty is for getting out of on-call. Work through these details when the partnership forms, and they are business decisions. Wait, and they become personal.

None of these special situations have to prevent the partnership from finding the fork in the road. However, they can make the process of getting there a struggle. It can simply take longer to get there or the partnership may never reach the maximum point of profitability. As long as the partnership's goal is to find the fork in the road, then managing through these challenges is no different than any other challenge previously mentioned. It goes back to communication, how decisions get made and money.

I have attempted to cover all other special challenges and situations in this chapter, but may have missed or didn't consider some. I encourage you to contact me if there is a challenge or situation you face that I have failed to address.

One final comment. I have not offered solutions or ideas on how to solve all of these challenges. The intent was to bring them to light and make you aware that they exist so you can determine whether they apply to your situation. If they do, then I encourage you to address them sooner rather than later. Don't wait till they happen, it will only make it more difficult to resolve.

Chapter 13
Early Warning Signs and Distress Signals

Every partnership has its challenges. Outside influences, personal issues and money concerns put stress on any relationship. Even the most rock-solid relationships go through difficult times. Don't expect your partnership to be any different. Otherwise, every time you face one of these rocky patches you'll wonder whether you should break up your partnership. Don't forget the purpose of your partnership is NOT to stay together forever. The purpose is to build your partnership so that it will end properly, to find the fork where the business has reached maximum profitability and satisfaction for those involved. Ending your partnership prematurely because of rough times in the relationship prevents you from achieving your partnership's purpose.

Breakdowns happen in all relationships, and partnerships are more subject to this than other businesses. I have said it before, but it's worth repeating: Problems do not go away simply because we chose to ignore them. They get uglier, hairier and more difficult to handle the longer they go on. When was the last time you pretended a problem didn't exist and it miraculously disappeared? It may have indeed gone away, but not without consequences. Don't disregard the warning signs and don't ignore the problems. Ignoring them will only make the relationship more challenging, which will not serve your objective of reaching your partnership goal.

Early Warning Signs: The Preventative Approach

1. **Disagreements occur more frequently.** There will never ever be a time when you and your partner agree on everything. Can't happen, period! However, if you find that more often than not you and your partner disagree about major things, it's time to take notice.

2. **Disagreements occur less frequently.** Some partnerships are built on strife and bickering. I don't recommend this, but I've seen partnerships that exist this way. Should this change and you find your partner saying, "Whatever you want," pay attention.

3. **Little things become big things.** Suddenly everything becomes a problem. Your partner begins to complain about everything, even the little things that seem unimportant. It may blow over, but don't assume that it will.

4. **Behavior changes become evident.** It might be something little, such as a partner showing up for work later and later. Maybe he misses a meeting or keeps the door to his office closed more frequently. If you notice behavior changes that continue for more than a month, it's time to have a conversation.

5. **Communication dries up.** Again watch for little signs. He or she quits asking your opinion, your daily lunches together become infrequent, the morning sit-downs are fewer and fewer. The signs may be subtle, but they'll be there if you pay attention.

6. **Complaints from employees.** If you start hearing complaints from employees, sit up and take notice. Employees are usually unlikely to complain about a partner to another partner. If they do, something is looming and you need to figure out what.

7. **More questions being asked.** Partners have the right to ask any questions they want. If, however, your partner is continually questioning every decision or sticking her nose into things she hadn't in the past, it's a warning sign. They are dissatisfied or concerned about something.

8. **You hear it through the grapevine.** A colleague or customer mentions something your partner said that you didn't know. Or you hear from someone that your partner is complaining, upset or angry. There's a reason he or she hasn't communicated directly with you. Find out what it is.

9. **Money frequently creeps into conversations.** Everyone wants to be adequately compensated. But if the topic of money creeps into most conversations, something's up.

This list is not meant to cover every possibility. Its primary goal is to get you thinking and noticing. We are all creatures of habit; if patterns change, there is a reason. I'm not suggesting the first time you notice something amiss you jump on it. What I'm suggesting is for you to pay attention and keep paying attention. A change in behavior, a pattern that changes, or something that continues to reoccur for a month or two is a warning sign. Numbness in your arm is not a sure sign you are headed for a stroke, and these warning signs aren't a guarantee the partnership is headed for failure. However, ignoring the numbness in your arm for an extended period of time is not prudent. The same applies to warning signs with your partnership.

CHECKLIST 19

How troubled is your partnership relationship?

1. What causes the most friction in your relationship?

☐ Lack of shared workload

☐ Lack of vision and goals agreement

☐ Lack of money

☐ Lack of partner's death

2. Which of the following most accurately describes your feelings?

☐ I want to drop my partner out of a third-story window

☐ I have visions of buying a shotgun and using it on my partner

☐ I dream of how easy my life would be if he would just go away

☐ Death is too good for him; I'd like him to be tortured

3. What would be the effect on the business if your partner were unable to work for three months?

☐ No one would notice his absence

☐ Everyone would notice his absence and celebrate

☐ No difference at all, I'm doing his job anyhow

☐ It would be a huge bonus. We'd be more productive without him

4. When there are problems, you and your partner …

☐ Work collaboratively to solve the problem

☐ Share responsibility for the problem and the solution

☐ Figure that responsibility is a one-way street, mine when things go wrong

☐ Fight like cats and dogs, throwing around accusations and blame

5. Discussion about work life balance always …

☐ Work out fine, we are in complete alignment

☐ End up 50-50 – all life balance is his and work is mine

☐ She doesn't show up for work, so we have no discussions

☐ His or her idea of work is the golf course, so what do you think

What Are the Indicators?

There are indicators that the partnership is in distress. Distress is more than the normal ups and downs you experience in any relationship. It's more than the fleeting thoughts you have of wanting to strangle your partner. Distress signals indicate the partnership is in serious trouble and requires intervention to put it back on track. One point I want you to accept: There are serious problems and discord in the partnership because you ignored the earlier warning signs. Sure, it's possible that something came out of the blue, but it's more likely that while you were busy building the business you turned a blind eye to the rumblings that eventually erupted into the crisis you are now facing.

You have to remember that when the partnership relationship is distressed, it will inevitably affect the business. And that affects your realizing your goal for the partnership. The ideal scenario is that major problems in your partnership never occur, but this is unlikely. We've already discussed that events and circumstances cause changes in people and the business. These changes can be significant and trigger a downward spiral in the relationship. The indicators are there and you don't have to look too hard to see them. And just as with warning signs, pretending these indicators don't exist doesn't make them go away.

1. **Communication breakdowns.** Communication breakdowns lead the list of signs that the partnership is in trouble. At the beginning of Chapter 8 I said, "Underlying everything that works and everything that doesn't in our personal and professional lives is communication." When communication breaks down you can expect a rough road ahead.

What suggests that communications are breaking down? Listening stops on both sides. Judgments and assumptions leak into every thought and conversation. Blame is rampant. Sarcasm is the norm and body language clearly says "this is your problem, not mine." Are you having the same conversations over and over again with no new results? Do you avoid difficult conversations because you feel they will end badly? How often do your conversations just end, without resolution? All of these signify that communication is a serious problem.

2. **Conflict becomes the norm.** Conflicts are more than disagreements or wanting to toss your partner out of the third-story window. When disagreements become knock-down, drag-out fights, they have escalated to conflict. Symptoms of conflict include: You find every discussion turns into a battle; there is no subject on which you see eye to eye; you're at odds with your partner about anything and everything; you find yourself wondering daily what you were thinking when you partnered with this person. This is conflict.

3. **Vision and goals are no longer in alignment.** When you came together as partners, the vision you had for the business was to build a partnership so that it reached its maximum point of profitability and satisfaction, allowing it to end properly. How you achieved this vision may not have been identical, but it was close enough. Now, you find that what you want and what your partner wants are worlds apart. This could relate to ideas on building or managing the business, direction of the company, work/life balance considerations … anything where you and your partner are at odds.

Depending on the specifics, some issues may be insurmountable. Sometimes your views are so far apart there is no place to compromise or meet in the middle. In the next chapter we'll address this.

4. **Increasing money problems.** Revenues and profits do not have a continuous straight line upward. They rise and fall throughout the life of a business. However, if money is increasingly a problem, you have a bigger problem than just money. It doesn't matter whether it's revenue or an expense issue: When the partnership is repeatedly and increasingly in a quandary about money, the partnership is in trouble.

5. **Control issues.** This may show up as conflict, but watch for indicators that the underlying issue is one of control. Someone isn't happy with the way things are going and wants to exert control. Decisions are questioned, information is requested about everything and your partner is attempting to operate in your area of responsibility. Something's more than just a little amiss.

6. **Continuous power struggles.** This is different from control. Power struggles aren't as likely to occur in a two-person partnership, but they will with partnerships of three or more. As the number of partners increases, so does the likelihood that power struggles will occur. It may initially appear as partners banding together to ensure a specific outcome on a decision. It escalates to groups of partners splintering from the rest, driving their own agenda and even one or more pushing for control of the business. People are people and there will always be differences of opinion and a desire to have it "my

way." When there is a power struggle or the balance of power is shifting, it indicates that partners are discontent and want change.

7. **Personal problems become front and center.** Everyone has personal problems. However, when a partner's personal problems become apparent to others and becomes the topic of conversation, there is big trouble brewing for the partnership and the business.

8. **Crisis management becomes SOP.** When crisis management becomes the only way problems are handled, it indicates a deep problem either with the partnership, the business or both. As a sweeping generalization, crisis management happens when there is a lack of trust, when money is an increasing problem or communication breakdowns are so severe that everything is viewed as potential crisis.

When a partnership relationship is in distress, it will affect the business. Assuming it won't is naïve and foolish. Assuming that things will get better if you ignore problems is idiotic. Go back to your goal … to finding the fork in the road. You won't reach this goal if you close your eyes to the early-warning signs and distress signals. Partners must recognize the warning signs and distress signals and respond to them quickly and vigilantly.

One point to keep in mind, some situations do not have an answer or resolution. In the next chapter we will be discussing options to consider when this occurs.

Chapter 14
When it's Over: Severing the Relationship

"By the time a partnership dissolves, it has dissolved."
— John Updike

Sometimes, no matter what you do, the relationship does not improve. This is not the time to cast blame. I encourage you to just believe that all parties did their best. The differences are simply too vast and the partnership needs to dissolve.

Remember that relationships change over time. What brought you and your partner together initially may no longer be true for you today. Needs change and people change. Both are good. However, these changes may suggest that there is not enough synergy between you and your partner to make the partnership succeed. Even if the business is a whopping success, it does not mean that the partnership relationship is a success. Just because the partnership relationship is not a success, it does not mean you or your partner are failures as people, in fact just the opposite. You can't have a successful business if the individuals running it are failures. All it indicates is that you and your partner have different needs and wants. The path you have each chosen has diverged and it's time to go your separate ways.

You may not have reached your partnership goal, but understand that when your needs and wants, individually or for the business, are vastly different from your partner's you won't reach the goal of finding the fork in the road. Concentrate now on moving on to the next step and severing the relationship as painlessly as possible. Your focus now has to be on yourself and what's best for you; what's best for the business takes a back seat.

Getting Past Hurt and Anger

There is no getting around this. When a relationship ends, even if it is clearly the right decision, it often does so with hurt and anger. We want someone to blame and of course it's going to be the other guy. Regardless of how the decision was made, even if it was your decision, you are going to suffer hurt feelings and anger. Expect these feelings and recognize they are part of the healing process.

But looking for retribution and retaliation is not part of the healing process. If that's what you are feeling, I suggest you seek professional help. These feelings are not healthy and they won't serve your efforts to move on to the next stage of your life. And the probability is that you can't and won't act on them. Should you choose to act on them, litigation is the likely outcome, which is costly to everyone on so many levels.

Understand and accept that some relationships won't succeed. Severing the partnership may end up being the best decision you ever make. It may just take time for you to recognize this. Often it is only retrospectively that we can understand why something happened or that a decision was correct. Give yourself time.

What Have You Learned?

Take the time to assess what you have learned from having a partner and the breakup of the relationship. There is always something to take away that is a valuable lesson for you and any future endeavors. What would you do differently the next time? What aspects would you like to re-create in another relationship or business? Do you want another partner? If so, what have you learned from your previous partnership that would serve you well in another partnership?

And consider what you have learned about yourself, not just the situation. This experience, regardless of how tumultuous or how it ended, offers you a key learning opportunity. Use it to help you determine what's next for you and as you move forward.

The Partner Who Stays and the Impact on the Business

When there has been constant conflict and friction, the dissolution of the partnership will likely have a positive effect on the business. Employees know what's going on and it affects them, even if you think it doesn't. As the partner who is staying, your focus and attention will no longer be divided between the business and dealing with the partnership challenges. Having a single focus has to be positive for the growth of the business.

Sometimes, the partner who is leaving held a key role. That role and area of responsibilities needs to be handled. This may put strain on the remaining partner or staff until a suitable replacement is found. It's important to recognize this is a short-term problem. Don't let it overwhelm you.

The final topic to address is what to communicate both internally and externally about a partner leaving or the dissolution of the partnership. What message do you want to deliver to staff and customers? It's important that the message convey confidence and excitement about the future. Staff may feel uncertain and question the stability of the company when a key partner leaves. Address this openly and honestly with employees. Customers may or may not be affected. If they had a close working relationship with the partner who left, assure them it's business as usual.

It's equally important to work out the details with your ex-partner about what he or she intends to tell people. You don't want to find yourself saying one thing about the situation and your ex-partner saying something completely different. You may not ultimately be able to control what he or she says, but at the very least have the conversation.

Severing a relationship is never easy, even when all parties agree it's the best outcome. If you are feeling hurt or angry, it's to be expected, and over time those feelings will dissipate. Also know that looking forward to what's next and moving on is the best decision you can make. Take what lessons you can from the experience. A wise man once told me that he learned if he spent all his time looking in his rear-view mirror, he would crash into the car in front of him. Don't spend all your time looking in your rear-view mirror. If you need time to heal, take it, but don't take too long.

Chapter 15
You've Found the Fork in the Road

Congratulations! Your vision for your partnership has been realized. You have reached the point of maximum profitability and satisfaction for the partners, and now you will be able to end it properly. Keep in mind that ending it properly does not connote that the business goes away or even that all partners go away. Let's take a look at some possible scenarios of "finding the fork in the road."

1. **Partner is bought out.** Sometimes one or more partners sell their equity to the remaining partner(s).

2. **Partner retires.** Consider medical practices, accounting firms and law practices: The business continues, but a partner retires. They have found their own personal fork. The same holds true for other businesses.

3. **Acquisition or merger.** Savvy business owners take advantage of opportunities. Merging with or acquiring a like business opens up possibilities that might not previously have existed.

4. **Business is sold.** The time has come for the partners to capitalize on the fruits of their labor and move on to the next adventure.

5. **Succession plan implemented.** The succession plan that was created is now implemented.

There are other scenarios in which a partner or even the business changes as a result of the partnership reaching its purpose. Congratulate yourself and your partners. The path to this point was not a straight line, but you kept going. You moved the barriers, weathered the ups and downs, broke new ground and created a wildly successful business partnership. Go take some time to celebrate. You deserve it.

In Conclusion

Building a successful business is a whole lot easier than creating a successful partnership. There is no easy path that ensures success in your relationship as partners. As I stated at the beginning of this book, in order for partnerships to flourish beyond being profitable, partners must explore how to create a shared vision, establish compatibility, apply ground rules, build durable relationships, foster trust, and measure progress along the way as well as determine how to handle change as a unit. This takes work, patience and long-term commitment to the goal that brought you together in the first place. The point was to build the business with the goal of finding the fork in the road, and when that happens you know it's time to end the partnership, and to end it properly.

I want to leave you with a final thought. It's about communication. I can't stress enough how critical communication is in your relationship. There are no guarantees in life or in business, but one thing I know for sure. Nothing kills a relationship more quickly than poor or ineffective communication. And nothing prevents you from finding the fork more than a soured relationship. Communication starts with listening and ends with a willingness to have the difficult conversations. Reread the quote by Francis Garagnon in Chapter 8;

I couldn't have said it better. Communication is the cornerstone of a successful relationship. It won't prevent problems or challenges, but it will make them easier to manage when they occur. And I'll bet that you'll also discover some problems never come up at all.

I wish you success with your business and, more importantly, with your partnership. You've taken a big step by reading this book. My hope is that you take some of the principles and ideas I have presented and use them to build a stronger partnership that is not only financially satisfying but personally satisfying to you. Here's to you and your partners finding the fork in the road.

Author Biography

There are loads of coaches and consultants who tout their ability to help companies get "ROI", but regardless of the growth strategy any professional brings to the table, the fact remains that the partners and the C-suite must be able to communicate effectively with each other and with people both inside and outside their company. So, while many organizational coaches and consultants may be able to come up with a strategy, Linda Finkle, CEO of Incedo Group, has over 25 years experience as an executive in her own company, working in both entrepreneurial and organizational settings, helping people change effectively. And her strategies reflect that experience.

LINDA FINKLE has been a business executive and partnership coach for over ten years. She has worked with dozens of partnerships and family business partnerships across a variety of industries. Finkle helps bring about changes in attitude, gets people listening, thinking, and communicating in new ways that have everyone climbing onboard for whatever changes are coming their way. Of course company profitability is an inevitable side effect but at least as important is partners and employees have more fun.

TreeNeutral